W.J. Widdelton

The Book of Ballads

A New Edition, with Serveral new Ballads

W.J. Widdelton

The Book of Ballads
A New Edition, with Serveral new Ballads

ISBN/EAN: 9783744768276

Printed in Europe, USA, Canada, Australia, Japan

Cover: Foto ©Thomas Meinert / pixelio.de

More available books at **www.hansebooks.com**

THE

BOOK OF BALLADS.

EDITED BY

BON GAULTIER.

A NEW EDITION, WITH SEVERAL NEW BALLADS

With Illustrations.

NEW YORK
W. J. WIDDLETON
SUCCESSOR TO J. S. REDFIELD
1862

CONTENTS.

Spanish Ballads.

American Ballads.

𝔐iscellaneous 𝔅allads.

CONTENTS. vii

MISCELLANEOUS BALLADS (continued):—

SPANISH BALLADS.

The Broken Pitcher.

It was a Moorish maiden was sitting by a well,
And what the maiden thought of, I cannot, cannot tell,
When by there rode a valiant knight from the town of
Oviedo—
Alphonzo Guzman was he hight, the Count of Desparedo.

"Oh, maiden, Moorish maiden? why sitt'st thou by the
spring?
Say, dost thou seek a lover, or any other thing?
Why gazest thou upon me, with eyes so large and
wide,
And wherefore doth the pitcher lie broken by thy
side?"

"I do not seek a lover, thou Christian knight so gay,
Because an article like that hath never come my way;
And why I gaze upon you, I cannot, cannot tell,
Except that in your iron hose you look uncommon
swell.

"My pitcher it is broken, and this the reason is,—
A shepherd came behind me, and tried to snatch a kiss,
I would not stand his nonsense, so ne'er a word I
      spoke,
But scored him on the costard, and so the jug was
      broke.

"My uncle, the Alcaydè, he waits for me at home,
And will not take his tumbler until Zorayda come.
I cannot bring him water—the pitcher is in pieces—
And so I'm sure to catch it, 'cos he wallops all his
      nieces."

"Oh, maiden, Moorish maiden! wilt thou be ruled
      by me!
So wipe thine eyes and rosy lips, and give me kisses
      three;
And I 'll give thee my helmet, thou kind and courteous
      lady,
To carry home the water to thy uncle, the Alcaydè."

He lighted down from off his steed—he tied him to a
      tree—
He bowed him to the maiden, and took his kisses three:
"To wrong thee, sweet Zorayda, I swear would be a
      sin!"
He knelt him at the fountain, and he dipped his helmet in.

Up rose the Moorish maiden—behind the knight she
      steals,
And caught Alphonzo Guzman up tightly by the heels;

She tipped him in, and held him down beneath the bub-
bling water,—
"Now, take thou that for venturing to kiss Al Hamet's
daughter!"

A Christian maid is weeping in the town of Oviedo;
She waits the coming of her love, the Count of Desparedo.
I pray you all in charity, that you will never tell,
How he met the Moorish maiden beside the lonely well.

. . '

Don Fernando Gomersalez.

FROM THE SPANISH OF ASTLEY'S.

.

Don Fernando Gomersalez! basely have they borne
    thee down;
Paces ten behind thy charger is thy glorious body
    thrown;
Fetters have they bound upon thee—iron fetters fast
    and sure;
Don Fernando Gomersalez, thou art captive to the Moor!

Long within a sable dungeon pined that brave and noble
    knight,
For the Saracenic warriors well they knew and feared
    his might;
Long he lay and long he languished on his dripping bed
    of stone,
Till the cankered iron fetters ate their way into his bone.

On the twentieth day of August—'t was the feast of
    false Mahound—
Came the Moorish population from the neighboring cities
    round;

There to hold their foul carousal, there to dance and
    there to sing,
And to pay their yearly homage to Al-Widdicomb, the
    King !

First they wheeled their supple coursers, wheeled them
    at their utmost speed,
Then they galloped by in squadrons, tossing far the light
    jereed ;
Then around the circus racing, faster than the swallow
    flies,
Did they spurn the yellow saw-dust in the rapt specta
    tors' eyes.

Proudly did the Moorish monarch every passing warrior
    greet,
As he sat enthroned above them, with the lamps beneath
    his feet;
" Tell me, thou black-bearded Cadi ! are there any in
    the land,
That against my janissaries dare one hour in combat
    stand ?"

Then the bearded Cadi answered—" Be not wrotn, my
    lord, the King,
If thy faithful slave shall venture to observe one little
    thing ;
Valiant, doubtless, are thy warriors, and their beards
    are long and hairy,
And a thunderbolt in battle is each bristly janissary :

" But I cannot, O my sovereign, quite forgot that fearful
    day,
When I saw the Christian army in its terrible array ;
When they charged across the footlights like a torrent
    down its bed,
With the red cross floating o'er them, and Fernando at
    their head !

" Don Fernando Gomersalez ! matchless chieftain he in
    war,
Mightier than Don Sticknejo, braver than the Cid
    Bavar !
Not a cheek within Grenada, O my King, but wan and
    pale is,
When they hear the dreaded name of Don Fernando
    Gomersalez !"

" Thou shalt see thy champion, Cadi ! hither quick the
    captive bring !"
Thus in wrath and deadly anger spoke Al-Widdicomb,
    the King ;
" Paler than a maiden's forehead is the Christian's hue I
    ween,
Since a year within the dungeons of Grenada he hath
    been !"

Then they brought the Gomersalez, and they led the
    warrior in,
Weak and wasted seemed his body, and his face was
    pale and thin ;

But the ancient fire was burning, unallayed, within his
    eye,
And his step was proud and stately, and his look was
    stern and high.

Scarcely from tumultuous cheering could the galleried
    crowd refrain,
For they knew Don Gomersalez and his prowess in the
    plain;
But they feared the grizzly despot and his myrmidons
    in steel,
So their sympathy descended in the fruitage of Seville.

"Wherefore, monarch, hast thou brought me from the
    dungeon dark and drear,
Where these limbs of mine have wasted in confinement
    for a year?
Dost thou lead me forth to torture?—Rack and pincers
    I defy—
Is it that thy base grotesquos may behold a hero
    die?"

"Hold thy peace, thou Christian caitiff! and attend to
    what I say:
Thou art called the starkest rider of the Spanish curs'
    array—
If thy courage be undaunted, as they say it was of
    yore,
Thou may'st yet achieve thy freedom,—yet regain thy
    native shore.

"Courses three within this circus 'gainst my warriors
  shalt thou run,
Ere yon weltering pasteboard ocean shall receive yon
  muslin sun;
Victor—thou shalt have thy freedom; but if stretched
  upon the plain,
To thy dark and dreary dungeon they shall bear thee
  back again."

"Give me but the armor, monarch, I have worn in many
  a field,
Give me but a trusty helmet, give me but my dinted
  shield;
And my old steed, Bavieca, swiftest courser in the
  ring,
And I rather should imagine that I'll do the business,
  King!"

Then they carried down the armor from the garret where
  it lay,
O! but it was red and rusty, and the plumes were shorn
  away;
And they led out Bavicca, from a foul and filthy van,
For the conqueror had sold him to a Moorish dogs-meat
  man.

When the steed beheld his master, then he whinned loud
  and free,
And, in token of subjection, knelt upon each broken
  knee;

And a tear of walnut largeness to the warrior's eyelids
 rose,
As he fondly picked a beanstraw from his coughing
 courser's nose.

"Many a time, O Bavieca, hast thou borne me through
 the fray!
Bear me but again as deftly through the listed ring this
 day;
Or if thou art worn and feeble, as may well have come
 to pass,
Time it is, my trusty charger, both of us were sent to
 grass!"

Then he seized his lance, and vaulting in the saddle, sate
 upright,
Marble seemed the noble courser, iron seemed the
 mailed knight;
And a cry of admiration burst from every Moorish
 lady—
" Five to four on Don Fernando!" cried the sable-
 bearded Cadi.

Warriors three from Alcantara burst into the listed space,
Warriors three, all bred in battle, of the proud Alham
 bra race:
Trumpets sounded, coursers bounded, and the foremost
 straight went down,
Tumbling, like a sack of turnips, just before the jeering
 Clown.

In the second chieftain galloped, and he bowed him to
    the King,
And his saddle-girths were tightened by the Master of
    the Ring;
Through three blazoned hoops he bounded ere the des-
    perate fight began—
Don Fernando! bear thee bravely!—'tis the Moor Ab-
    dorrhoman!

Like a double streak of lightning, clashing in the sul-
    phurous sky,
Met the pair of hostile heroes, and they made the saw-
    dust fly;
And the Moslem spear so stiffly smote on Don Fernan-
    do's mail,
That he reeled, as if in liquor, back to Bavieca's tail.

But he caught the mace beside him, and he griped it
    hard and fast,
And he swung it starkly upwards as the foeman bound-
    ed past;
And the deadly stroke descended through the skull and
    through the brain,
As ye may have seen a poker cleave a cocoa-nut in
    twain.

Sore astonished was the monarch, and the Moorish war-
    riors all,
Save the third bold chief, who tarried and beheld his
    brethren fall;

And the Clown in haste arising from the footstool where
    he set,
Notified the first appearance of the famous Acrobat!

Never on a single charger rides that stout and stalwart
    Moor,
Five beneath his stride so stately bear him o'er the
    trembling floor;
Five Arabians, black as midnight—on their necks the
    rein he throws,
And the outer and the inner feel the pressure of his
    toes.

Never wore that chieftain armor; in a knot himself he
    ties,
With his grizzly head appearing in the centre of his
    thighs.
Till the petrified spectator asks in paralyzed alarm—
Where may be the warrior's body,—which is leg, and
    which is arm?

"Sound the charge!" the coursers started; with a yell
    and furious vault,
High in air the Moorish champion cut a wondrous
    somersault;
O'er the head of Don Fernando like a tennis-ball he
    sprung,
Caught him tightly by the girdle, and behind the crup-
    per hung. .

Then his dagger Don Fernando plucked from out its
    jewelled sheath,
And he struck the Moor so fiercely, as he grappled him
    beneath,
That the good Damascus weapon sunk within the folds
    of fat,
And, as dead as Julius Cæsar, dropped the Gordian
    Acrobat.

Meanwhile, fast the sun was sinking,—it had sunk be-
    neath the sea,
Ere Fernando Gomersalez smote the latter of the three;
And Al-Widdicomb, the monarch, pointed with a bitter
    smile,
To the deeply-darkening canvass—blacker grew it all
    the while.

"Thou hast slain my warriors, Spaniard! but thou hast
    not kept thy time;
Only two had sunk before thee ere I heard the curfew
    chime;
Back thou goest to thy dungeon, and thou may'st be
    wondrous glad,
That thy head is on thy shoulders for thy work to-day,
    my lad!

"Therefore, all thy boasted valor, Christian dog, of no
    avail is!"
Dark as midnight grew the brow of Don Fernando
    Gomersalez;—

Stiffly sate he in his saddle, grimly looked around the
    ring,
Laid his lance within the rest, and shook his gauntlet at
    the King.

" O, thou foul and faithless traitor! wouldst thou play
    me false again ?
Welcome death and welcome torture, rather than the
    captive's chain !
But I give thee warning. caitiff !   Look thou sharply to
    thine eye—
Unavenged, at least in harness, Gomersalez shall not
    die !"

Thus he spoke, and Bavieca like an arrow forward flew,
Right and left the Moorish squadron wheeled to let the
    hero through ;
Brightly gleamed the light of vengeance—fiercely sped
    the fatal thrust—
From his throne the Moorish monarch tumbled lifeless
    in the dust.

Speed thee, speed thee, Bavieca ! speed thee faster than
    the wind !
Life and freedom are before thee, deadly foes give chase
    behind !
Speed thee up the sloping spring-board ; o'er the bridge
    that spans the seas ;
Yonder gauzy moon will light thee through the grove of
    canvas trees.

Close before thee, Pampeluna spreads her painted paste-
    board gate !
Speed thee onward, gallant courser, speed thee with thy
    knightly freight—
Victory ! the town receives them !—Gentle ladies, this
  . the tale is,
Which I learned in Astley's Circus, of Fernando Gomer-
    salez !

The Courtship of our Cid.

WHAT a pang of sweet emotion
    Thrilled the Master of the Ring,
When he first beheld the lady,
    Through the stabled portal spring!
Midway in his wild grimacing
    Stopped the piebald-visaged Clown:
And the thunders of the audience
    Nearly brought the gallery down

Donna Inez Woolfordinez!
    Saw ye ever such a maid,
With the feathers swaling o'er her,
    And her spangled rich brocade?
In her fairy hand a horsewhip,
    On her foot a buskin small,
So she stepped, the stately damsel,
    Through the scarlet grooms and all.

And she beckoned for her courser,
    And they brought a milk-white mare;
Proud. I ween, was that Arabian
    Such a gentle freight to bear:
2

And the Master moved towards her,
   With a proud and stately walk ;
And, in reverential homage,
   Rubbed her soles with virgin chalk.

Round she flew, as Flora flying
   Spans the circle of the year;
And the youth of London sighing,
   Half forgot the ginger beer—
Quite forgot the maids beside them ;
   As they surely well might do,
When she raised two Roman candles,
   Shooting fireballs red and blue !

Swifter than the Tartar's arrow,
   Lighter than the lark in flight,
On the left foot now she bounded,
   Now she stood upon the right.
Like a beautiful Bacchante,
   Here she soars, and there she kneels,
While amid her floating tresses,
   Flash two whirling Catherine wheels !

Hark ! the blare of yonder trumpet !
   See the gates are open wide !
Room, there, room for Gomersalez,—
   Gomersalez in his pride !
Rose the shouts of exultation,
   Rose the cat's triumphant call,
As he bounded, man and courser,
   Over Master, Clown, and all !

Donna Inez Woolfordinez!
  Why those blushes on thy cheek?
Doth thy trembling bosom tell thee,
  He hath come thy love to seek?
Fleet thy Arab—but behind thee
  He is rushing like a gale;
One foot on his coal black's shoulders,
  And the other on his tail!

Onward, onward, panting maiden!
  He is faint and fails—for now,
By the feet he hangs suspended
  From his glistening saddle-bow.
Down are gone both cap and feather,
  Lance and gonfalon are down!
Trunks, and cloak, and vest of velvet,
  He has flung them to the Clown.

Faint and failing! Up he vaulteth,
  Fresh as when he first began;
All in coat of bright vermilion,
  'Quipped as Shaw, the Life-guardsman.
Right and left his whizzing broadsword,
  Like a sturdy flail, he throws;
Cutting out a path unto thee
  Through imaginary foes.

Woolfordinez! speed thee onward!
  He is hard upon thy track,—
Paralyzed is Widdicombez,
  Nor his whip can longer crack;

He has flung away his broadsword,
   'Tis to clasp thee to his breast.
Onward!—see he bares his bosom,
   Tears away his scarlet vest;

Leaps from out his nether garments,
   And his leathern stock unties—
As the flower of London's dustmen,
   Now in swift pursuit he flies.
Nimbly now he cuts and shuffles,
   O'er the buckle, heel and toe!
And with hands deep in his pockets
   Winks to all the throng below!

Onward, onward rush the coursers;
   Woolfordinez, peerless girl,
O'er the garters lightly bounding
   From her steed with airy whirl!
Gomersalez, wild with passion,
   Danger—all but her—forgets;
Wheresoe'er she flies, pursues her,
   Casting clouds of somersets!

Onward, onward rush the coursers;
   Bright is Gomersalez' eye;
Saints protect thee, Woolfordinez,
   For his triumph, sure, is nigh!
Now his courser's flanks he lashes,
   O'er his shoulder flings the rein,
And his feet aloft he tosses,
   Holding stoutly by the mane!

Then his feet once more regaining,
  Doffs his jacket, doffs his smalls;
And in graceful folds around him
  A bespangled tunic falls.
Pinions from his heels are bursting,
  His bright locks have pinions o'er them;
And the public sees with rapture
  Maia's nimble son before them.

Speed thee, speed thee, Woolfordinez!
  For a panting god pursues;
And the chalk is very nearly
  Rubbed from thy white satin shoes;
Every bosom throbs with terror,
  You might hear a pin to drop;
All was hushed, save where a starting
  Cork gave out a casual pop.

One smart lash across his courser,
  One tremendous bound and stride,
And our noble Cid was standing
  By his Woolfordinez' side!
With a god's embrace he clasped her,
  Raised her in his manly arms;
And the stables' closing barriers
  Hid his valor, and her charms!

AMERICAN BALLADS.

The Fight with the Snapping Turtle.

OR, THE AMERICAN ST. GEORGE.

FYTTE FIRST.

HAVE you heard of Philip Slingsby,
   Slingsby of the manly chest;
How he slew the Snapping Turtle
   In the regions of the West?

Every day the huge Cawana
   Lifted up its monstrous jaws;
And it swallowed Langton Bennett,
   And digested Rufus Dawes.

Riled, I ween, was Philip Slingsby,
   Their untimely deaths to hear;
For one author owed him money,
   And the other loved him dear.

" Listen, now, sagacious Tyler,
    Whom the loafers all obey;
What reward will Congress give me,
    If I take this pest away ?"

Then sagacious Tyler answered,
    " You're the ring-tailed squealer!   Less
Than a hundred heavy dollars
    Won't be offered you, I guess!

" And a lot of wooden nutmegs
    In the bargain, too, we'll throw—
Only you just fix the criter—
    Won't you liquor ere you go?"

Straightway leaped the valiant Slingsby
    Into armor of Seville,
With a strong Arkansas toothpick
    Screwed in every joint of steel.

" Come thou with me, Cullen Bryant,
    Come with me as squire, I pray;
Be the Homer of the battle
    That I go to wage to-day."

So they went along careering
    With a loud and martial tramp,
Till they neared the Snapping Turtle
    In the dreary Swindle Swamp.

But when Slingsby saw the water,
    Somewhat pale, I ween, was he.
" If I come not back, dear Bryant,
    Tell the tale to Melanie!

"Tell her that I died devoted,
    Victim to a noble task !
Ha'n't you got a drop of brandy
    In the bottom of your flask ?"

As he spoke, an alligator
    Swam across the sullen creek;
And the two Columbians started
    When they heard the monster shriek :

For a snout of huge dimensions
    Rose above the waters high,
And took down the alligator,
    As a trout takes down a fly.

" 'Tarnal death! the Snapping Turtle!"
    Thus the squire in terror cried;
But the noble Slingsby straightway
    Drew the toothpick from his side.

" Fare thee well !" he cried, and dashing
    Through the waters, strongly swam :
Meanwhile Cullen Bryant, watching,
    Breathed a prayer and sucked a dram.

Sudden from the slimy bottom
    Was the snout again upreared,
With a snap as loud as thunder,—
    And the Slingsby disappeared.

Like a mighty steam-ship foundering,
    Down the monstrous vision sank ;
And the ripple, slowly rolling,
    Plashed and played upon the bank.

Still and stiller grew the water,
    Hushed the canes within the brake;
There was but a kind of coughing
    At the bottom of the lake.

Bryant wept as loud and deeply
    As a father for a son—
" He's a finished 'coon, is Slingsby,
    And the brandy's nearly done !"

FYTTE SECOND.

In a trance of sickening anguish,
    Cold, and stiff, and sore and damp,
For two days did Bryant linger
    By the dreary Swindle Swamp;

Always peering at the water,
    Always waiting for the hour,
When those monstrous jaws should open
    As he saw them ope before.

Still in vain;—the alligators
    Scrambled through the marshy brake,
And the vampire leeches gaily
    Sucked the garfish in the lake.

But the Snapping Turtle never
    Rose for food or rose for rest,
Since he lodged the steel deposit
    In the bottom of his chest.

2*

Only always from the bottom
    Violent sounds of coughing rolled,
Just as if the huge Cawana
    Had a most confounded cold.

On the bank lay Cullen Bryant,
    As the second moon arose;
Gouging on the sloping green sward
    Some imaginary foes.

When the swamp began to tremble
    And the canes to rustle fast,
As if some stupendous body
    Through their roots was crushing past.

And the water boiled and bubbled,
    And in groups of twos and threes,
Several alligators bounded,
    Smart as squirrels up the trees.

Then a hideous head was lifted,
    With such huge distended jaws,
That they might have held Goliath
    Quite as well as Rufus Dawes.

Paws of elephantine thickness
    Dragged its body from the bay,
And it glared at Cullen Bryant
    In a most unpleasant way.

Then it writhed as if in torture,
    And it staggered to and fro;
And its very shell was shaken,
    In the anguish of its throe:

And its cough grew loud and louder,
  And its sob more husky thick;
For, indeed, it was apparent
  That the beast was very sick.

Till at last a violent vomit
  Shook its carcass through and through,
And, as if from out a cannon,
  All in armor Slingsby flew.

Bent and bloody was the bowie,
  Which he held within his grasp;
And he seemed so much exhausted
  That he scarce had strength to gasp—

"Gouge him, Bryant! darn ye, gouge him!
  Gouge him while he's on the shore!"
And his thumbs were straightway buried
  Where no thumbs had pierced before.

Right from out their bony sockets,
  Did he scoop the monstrous balls;
And, with one convulsive shudder,
  Dead the Snapping Turtle falls!

       *   *   *   *

"Post the tin, sagacious Tyler!"
  But the old experienced file,
Leering first at Clay and Webster,
  Answered, with a quiet smile—

Since you dragged the 'tarnal crittur
From the bottom of the ponds,
Here's the hundred dollars due you,
All in Pennsylvanian Bonds!"

"**The only Good American Securities.**"

The Lay of Mr. Colt. -

[THE story of Mr. Colt, of which our Lay contains merely the sequel, is this: A New York printer, of the name of Adams, had the effrontery to call upon him one day for the payment of an account, which the independent Colt settled by cutting his creditor's head to fragments with an axe. He then packed his body in a box, sprinkling it with salt, and despatched it to a packet, bound for New Orleans. Suspicions having been excited, he was seized, and tried before Judge Kent. The trial is, perhaps, the most disgraceful upon the records of any country. The ruffian's mistress was produced in court, and examined in disgusting detail, as to her connexion with Colt, and his movements during the days and nights succeeding the murder. The head of the murdered man was bandied to and fro in the court, handed up to the jury, and commented on by witnesses and counsel; and to crown the horrors of the whole proceeding, the wretch's own counsel, a Mr. Emmet, commencing the defence with a cool admission that his client took the life of Adams, and following it up by a detail of the whole circumstances of this most brutal murder in the first person, as though he himself had been the murderer, ended by telling the jury, that his client was *"entitled to the sympathy of a jury of his country,"* as *"a young man just entering into life, whose prospects, probably have been permanently blasted."* Colt was found guilty; but a variety of exceptions were taken to the charge by the judge, and after a long series of appeals, which *occupied more than a year from the date of the conviction,* the sentence of death was ratified by Governor Seward. The rest of Colt's story is told in our ballad.]

STREAK THE FIRST.

*   *   *   *

AND now the sacred rite was done, and the marriage
    knot was tied,
And Colt withdrew his blushing wife a little way aside;

"Let 's go," he said, "into my cell, let 's go alone, my
    dear;
I fain would shelter that sweet face from the sheriff's
    odious leer.
The gaoler and the hangman, they are waiting both for
    me,—
I cannot bear to see them wink so knowingly at thee!
Oh, how I loved thee, dearest! They say that I am
    wild,
That a mother dares not trust me with the weasand of
    her child,
They say my bowie knife is keen to sliver into halves
The carcass of my enemy, as butchers slay their calves.
They say that I am stern of mood, because, like salted
    beef,
I packed my quartered foreman up, and marked him
    ' prime tariff;'
Because I thought to palm him on the simple-souled John
    Bull,
And clear a small per centage on the sale at Liverpool;
It may be so, I do not know—these things, perhaps, may
    be;
But surely I have always been a gentleman to thee!
Then come, my love, into my cell, short bridal space is
    ours,—
Nay, sheriff, never look thy watch—I guess there's good
    two hours.
We 'll shut the prison doors and keep the gaping world
    at bay,
For love is long as 'tarnity, though I must die to-day!"

STREAK THE SECOND.

THE clock is ticking onward,
   It nears the hour of doom,
And no one yet hath entered
   Into that ghastly room.
The gaoler and the sheriff
   They are walking to and fro;
And the hangman sits upon the steps,
   And smokes his pipe below.
In grisly expectation
   The prison all is bound,
And save expectoration,
   You cannot hear a sound.
The turnkey stands and ponders,
   His hand upon the bolt,—
"In twenty minutes more, I guess,
   'T will all be up with Colt!"
But see, the door is opened!
   Forth comes the weeping bride;
The courteous sheriff lifts his hat,
   And saunters to her side,—
"I beg your pardon, Mrs. C.,
   But is your husband ready?"
"I guess you'd better ask himself,"
   Replied the woful lady.

The clock is ticking onward,
   The minutes almost run,
The hangman's pipe is nearly out,
   'T is on the stroke of one.

At every grated window
  Unshaven faces glare;
There's Puke, the judge of Tennessee,
  And Lynch, of Delaware;
And Batter, with the long black beard,
  Whom Hartford's maids know well;
And Winkinson, from Fish Kill Reach,
  The pride of New Rochelle;
Elkanah Nutts, from Tarry Town,
  The gallant gouging boy;
And coon-faced Bushwhack, from the hills
  That frown o'er modern Troy;
Young Wheezer, whom our Willis loves,
  Because, 't is said, that he,
One morning from a bookstall filched
  The tale of "Melanie;"
And Skunk, who fought his country's fight
  Beneath the stripes and stars,—
All thronging at the windows stood,
  And gazed between the bars.

The little boys that stood behind
  (Young thievish imps were they!)
Displayed considerable *nous*
  On that eventful day;
For bits of broken looking-glass
  They held aslant on high,
And there a mirrored gallows-tree
  Met their delighted eye.*

*A Fact.

The clock is ticking onward;
　Hark! Hark! it striketh one!
Each felon draws a whistling breath,
　"Time's up with Colt; he's done!"

The sheriff looks his watch again,
　Then puts it in his fob,
And turns him to the hangman,—
　"Get ready for the job."
The gaoler knocketh loudly,
　The turnkey draws the bolt.
And pleasantly the sheriff says,
　"We're waiting, Mister Colt!"

No answer? No! no answer!
　All's still as death within;
The sheriff eyes the gaoler,
　The gaoler strokes his chin.
"I should n't wonder, Nahum, if
　It were as you suppose."
The hangman looked unhappy, and
　The turnkey blew his nose.

They entered. On his pallet
　The noble convict lay,—
The bridegroom on his marriage bed,
　But not in trim array.
His red right hand a razor held,
　Fresh sharpened from the hone,
And his ivory neck was severed,
　And gashed into the bone.

*　　*　　*　　*

And when the lamp is lighted
  In the long November days,
And lads and lasses mingle
  At the shucking of the maize;
When pies of smoking pumpkin
  Upon the table stand,
And bowls of black molasses
  Go round from hand to hand;
When slap-jacks, maple-sugared,
  Are hissing in the pan,
And cider, with a dash of gin,
  Foams in the social can;
When the good man wets his whistle,
  And the good wife scolds the child;
And the girls exclaim convulsively,
  "Have done, or I'll be riled!"
When the loafer sitting next them
  Attempts a sly caress,
And whispers, "Oh! you 'possum,
  You 've fixed my heart, I guess!"
With laughter and with weeping,
  Then shall they tell the tale,
How Colt his foreman quartered,
  And died within the gaol.

The Death Of Jabez Dollar.

[Before the following poem, which originally appeared in " Fraser's Magazine," could have reached America, intelligence was received in this country of an affray in Congress, very nearly the counterpart of that which the Author has here imagined in jest. It was very clear, to any one who observed the state of public manners in America, that such occurrences *must* happen sooner or later. The Americans apparently felt the force of the satire, as the poem was widely reprinted throughout the States. It subsequently returned to this country, embodied in an American work on American manners, where it characteristically appeared as the writer's *own* production; and it afterwards went the round of British newspapers, as an amusing satire by an American, of his countrymen's foibles!]

THE Congress met, the day was wet, Van Buren took
    the chair,
On either side, the statesman pride of fair Kentuck was
    there.
With moody frown, there sat Calhoun, and slowly in
    his cheek
His quid he thrust, and slaked the dust, as Webster
    rose to speak.

Upon that day, near gifted Clay, a youthful member sat,
And like a free American upon the floor he spat;
Then turning round to Clay, he said, and wiped his
    manly chin,
" What kind of Locofoco's that, as wears the painter's
    skin?"

" Young man," quoth Clay, "avoid the way of Slick
    of Tennessee,
Of gougers fierce, the eyes that pierce, the fiercest
    gouger he.
He chews and spits as there he sits, and whittles at the
    chairs,
And in his hand, for deadly strife, a bowie-knife he
    bears.

"Avoid that knife! In frequent strife its blade, so long
    and thin,
Has found itself a resting-place his rival's ribs within."
But coward fear came never near young Jabez Dollar's
    heart,
"Were he an alligator, I would rile him pretty
    smart!"

Then up he rose, and cleared his nose, and looked toward
    the chair,
He saw the stately stripes and stars—our country's flag
    was there!
His heart beat high, with savage cry upon the floor he
    sprang,
Then raised his wrist, and shook his fist, and spoke his
    first harangue.

" Who sold the nutmegs made of wood—the clocks that
    wouldn't figure ?
Who grinned the bark off gum-trees dark,—the ever-
    lasting nigger ?

For twenty cents, ye Congress gents, through 'tarnity
    I'll kick
That man, I guess, though nothing less than coon-faced
    Colonel Slick!"

The colonel smiled—with frenzy wild,—his very beard
    waxed blue,—
His shirt it could not hold him, so wrathy riled he
    grew;
He foams and frets, his knife he whets upon his seat
    below—
He sharpens it on either side, and whittles at his toe,—

"Oh! waken, snakes, and walk your chalks!" he cried,
    with ire elate;
" Darn my old mother, but I will in wild cats whip my
    weight!
Oh! 'tarnal death I'll spoil your breath, young Dollar,
    and your chaffing,—
Look to your ribs, for here is that will tickle them with-
    out laughing!"

His knife he raised—with fury crazed, he sprang across
    the hall;
He cut a caper in the air—he stood before them all:
He never stopped to look or think if he the deed should
    do,
But spinning sent the President, and on young Dollar
    flew.

They met—they closed—they sunk—they rose,—in vain
    young Dollar strove—
For, like a streak of lightning greased, the infuriate
    colonel drove
His bowie blade deep in his side, and to the ground
    they rolled,
And, drenched in gore, wheeled o'er and o'er, locked in
    other's hold.

With fury dumb—with nail and thumb—they struggled
    and they thrust,—
The blood ran red from Dollar's side, like rain, upon
    the dust;
He nerved his might for one last spring, and as he sunk
    and died,
Reft of an eye, his enemy fell groaning at his side.

Thus did he fall within the hall of Congress, that brave
    youth;
The bowie-knife had quenched his life of valor and of
    truth;
And still among the statesmen throng at Washington
    they tell
How nobly Dollar gouged his man—how gallantly he
    fell!

The Alabama Duel.

"Young chaps, give ear,—the case is clear. You, Silas
    Fixings, you
Pay Mister Nehemiah Dodge, them dollars as you 're
    due,
You are a bloody cheat,—you are. But spite of all
    your tricks, it
Is not in you, Judge Lynch to do. No! no how you
    can fix it!"

Thus spake Judge Lynch, as there he sat in Alabama's
    forum,
Around he gazed with legs upraised upon the bench high
    o'er him;
And, as he gave this sentence stern to him who stood
    beneath,
Still, with his gleaming bowie-knife he slowly picked his
    teeth.

It was high noon, the month was June, and sultry was
    the air,
A cool gin-sling stood by his hand, his coat hung o'er
    his chair;
All naked were his manly arms, and, shaded by his hat,
Like an old Senator of Rome, that simple Archon sat.

" A bloody cheat ?—Oh, legs and feet !" in wrath young
    Silas cried ;
And, springing high into the air, he jerked his quid
    aside.—
" No man shall put my dander up, or with my feelings
    trifle,
As long as Silas Fixings wears a bowie-knife and rifle."

" If your shoes pinch," replied Judge Lynch, " you 'll
    very soon have ease,
I 'll give you satisfaction, squire, in any way you
    please ;
Where are your weapons ?—knife or gun ?—at both I 'm
    pretty spry !"
" Oh ! 'tarnal death, you 're spry, you are ?" quoth
    Silas ; " so am I !"

Hard by the town a forest stands, dark with the shades
    of time,
And they have sought that forest dark at morning's
    early prime ;
Lynch, backed by Nehemiah Dodge, and Silas with a
    friend,
And half the town in glee came down, to see that con-
    test's end.

They led their men two miles apart, they measured out
    the ground ;
A belt of that vast wood it was, they notched the trees
    around ;

Into the tangled brake they turned them off, and neither
    knew
Where he should seek his wagered foe, how get him into
    view.

With stealthy tread, and stooping head, from tree to
    tree they passed,
They crept beneath the crackling furze, they held their
    rifles fast:
Hour passed on hour, the noon-day sun smote fiercely
    down, but yet
No sound to the expectant crowd proclaimed that they
    had met.

And now the sun was going down, when, hark! a rifle's
    crack!
Hush—hush! another strikes the air, and all their breath
    drew back,—
Then crashing on through bush and briar, the crowd from
    either side
Rushed in to see whose rifle sure with blood the moss
    had dyed.

Weary with watching up and down, brave Lynch con-
    ceived a plan,
An artful dodge whereby to take at unawares his
    man;
He hung his hat upon a bush, and hid himself
    hard by,
Young Silas thought he had him fast, and at the hat
    let fly.

3

It fell; up sprung young Silas,—he hurled his gun away;
Lynch fixed him with his rifle from the ambush where
  he lay.
The bullet pierced his manly breast—yet, valiant to the
  last,
He drew his fatal bowie-knife, and up his foxtail* cast.

With tottering steps and glazing eye he cleared the space
  between,
And stabbed the air as, in Macbeth, still stabs the
  younger Kean ;
Brave Lynch received him with a bang that stretched
  him on the ground,
Then sat himself serenely down till all the crowd drew
  round.

They hailed him with triumphant cheers—in him each
  loafer saw
The bearing bold that could uphold the majesty of law ;
And, raising him aloft, they bore him homewards at his
  ease,—
That noble judge, whose daring hand enforced his own
  decrees.

They buried Silas Fixings in the hollow where he fell,
And gum-trees wave above his grave—that tree he loved
  so well;
And the 'coons sit chattering o'er him when the nights
  are long and damp,
But he sleeps well in that lonely dell, the Dreary
  'Possum Swamp.

* The Yankee substitute for the *chapeau de soie*.

The American's Apostrophe to Boz.

[Rapidly as oblivion does its work now-a-days, the burst of amiable indignation with which enlightened America received the issue of Boz's "Notes," can scarcely yet be forgotten. Not content with waging a universal rivalry in the piracy of the work, Columbia showered upon its author the riches of its own choice vocabulary of abuse; while some of her more fiery spirits threw out playful hints as to the propriety of gouging the "strannger," and furnishing him with a permanent suit of tar and feathers, in the very improbable event of his paying them a second visit. The perusal of these animated expressions of free opinion suggested the following lines, which those who remember Boz's book, and the festivities with which he was all but hunted to death, will at once understand. We hope we have done justice to the bitterness and "immortal hate" of these thin-skinned sons of freedom.]

SNEAK across the wide Atlantic, worthless London's
    puling child,
Better that its waves should bear thee, than the land
    thou hast reviled;
Better in the stifling cabin, on the sofa should'st thou
    lie,
Sickening as the fetid nigger bears the greens and bacon
    by.
Better, when the midnight horrors haunt the strained
    and creaking ship,
Thou should'st yell in vain for brandy with a fever-
    sodden lip;

When amid the deepening darkness and the lamp's
    expiring shade,
From the bagman's berth above thee comes the boun-
    tiful cascade.
Better than upon the Broadway thou should'st be at
    noon-day seen,
Smirking like a Tracy Tupman with a Mantalini mien,
With a rivulet of satin falling o'er thy puny chest,
Worse than even N. P. Willis for an evening party
    dressed !

We received thee warmly—kindly—though we knew
    thou wert a quiz,
Partly for thyself it may be, chiefly for the sake of
    Phiz!
Much we bore and much we suffered, listening to
    remorseless spells
Of that Smike's unceasing drivellings, and these ever-
    lasting Nells.
When you talk of babes and sunshine, fields, and all
    that sort of thing,
Each Columbian inly chuckled, as he slowly sucked his
    sling ;
And though all our sleeves were bursting, from the
    many hundreds near,
Not one single scornful titter rose on thy complacent ear.

Then to show thee to the ladies, with our usual want of
    sense
We engaged the place in Park Street at a ruinous
    expense ;

Ev'n our own three-volumed Cooper waived his old pre-
scriptive right,
And deluded Dickens figured first on that eventful
night.
Clusters of uncoated Yorkers, vainly striving to be cool,
Saw thee desperately plunging through the perils of La
Poule;
And their muttered exclamation drowned the tenor of
the tune,—
"Don't he beat all natur hollow? Don't he foot it like
a ' coon ? "

Did we spare our brandy-cocktails, stint thee of our
whisky-grogs?
Half the juleps that we gave thee would have floored a
Newman Noggs ;
And thou took'st them in so kindly, little was there then
to blame,
To thy parched and panting palate sweet as mother's
milk they came.
Did the hams of old Virginny find no favor in thine
eyes?
Came no soft compunction o'er thee at the thought of
pumpkin pies ?
Could not all our care and coddling teach thee how to
draw it mild?
But, no matter, we deserve it. Serves us right! We
spoilt the child!

You, forsooth, must come crusading, boring us with
broadest hints
Of your own peculiar losses by American reprints.

Such an impudent remonstrance never in our face was
    flung;
Lever stands it, so does Ainsworth; *you*, I guess, may
    hold your tongue.
Down our throats you'd cram your projects, thick and
    hard as pickled salmon,
That, I s'pose, you call free-trading, I pronounce it utter
    gammon.
No, my lad, a cuter vision than your own might soon
    have seen,
That a true Columbian ogle carries little that is green.
Quite enough we pay, I reckon, when we stump a cent
    or two
For the voyages and travels of a freshman such as you.

I have been at Niagara, I have stood beneath the
    Falls,
I have marked the water twisting over its rampagious
    walls;
But "a holy calm sensation," one, in fact, of perfect
    peace,
Was as much my first idea as the thought of Christmas
    geese.
As for "old familiar faces," looking through the misty
    air,
Surely you were strongly liquored when you saw your
    Chuckster there.
One familiar face, however, you will very likely see,
If you'll only treat the natives to a call in Tennessee,
Of a certain individual, true Columbian every inch,
In a high judicial station, called by 'mancipators, Lynch.

Half-an-hour of conversation with his worship in a wood
Would, I strongly notion, do you an infernal deal of
good.
Then you'd understand more clearly than you ever did
before,
Why an independent patriot freely spits upon the floor,
Why he gouges when he pleases, why he whittles at the
chairs,
Why for swift and deadly combat still the bowie-knife
he bears:—
Why he sneers at the Old Country with republican
disdain,
And, unheedful of the negro's cry, still tighter draws his
chain.
All these things the judge shall teach thee of the land
thou hast reviled;
Get thee o'er the wide Atlantic, worthless London's
puling child!

MISCELLANEOUS BALLADS.

The Student of Jena.

Once,—'t was when I lived at Jena,—
  At a Wirthshaus' door I sat;
And in pensive contemplation,
  Eat the sausage thick and fat;
Eat the kraut, that never sourer
  Tasted to my lips than here;
Smoked my pipe of strong canaster,
  Sipped my fifteenth jug of beer;
Gazed upon the glancing river,
  Gazed upon the tranquil pool,
Whence the silver-voiced Undine,
  When the nights were calm and cool,
As the Baron Fouqué tells us,
  Rose from out her shelly grot,
Casting glamor o'er the waters,
  Witching that enchanted spot.
From the shadow which the coppice
  Flings across the rippling stream,

Did I hear a sound of music—
Was it thought or was it dream?
There, beside a pile of linen,
Stretched along the daised sward, —
Stood a young and blooming maiden—
'T was her thrush-like song I heard,
Evermore within the eddy
Did she plunge the white chemise;
And her robes were loosely gathered
Rather far above her knees;
Then my breath at once forsook me,
For too surely did I deem
That I saw the fair Undine
Standing in the glancing stream—
And I felt the charm of knighthood;
And from that remembered day,
Every evening to the Wirthshaus
Took I my enchanted way.
Shortly to relate my story,
Many a week of summer long,
Came I there, when beer-o'ertaken,
With my lute and with my song;
Sang in mellow-toned soprano,
All my love and all my wo,
Till the river-maiden answered,
Lilting in the stream below:—
"Fair Undine! sweet Undine!
Dost thou love as I love thee?"
"Love is free as running water,"
Was the answer made to me.

Thus, in interchange seraphic,
  Did I woo my phantom fay,
Till the nights grew long and chilly,
  Short and shorter grew the day;
Till at last—'t was dark and gloomy,
  Dull and starless was the sky,
And my steps were all unsteady,
  For a little flushed was I,—
To the well accustomed signal
  No response the maiden gave;
But I heard the waters washing,
  And the moaning of the wave.

Vanished was my own Undine,
  All her linen, too, was gone;
And I walked about, lamenting,
  On the river bank alone.

Idiot that I was, for never
  Had I asked the maiden's name.
Was it Lieschen—was it Gretchen?
  Had she tin—or whence she came?

So I took my trusty meerschaum,
  And I took my lute likewise;
Wandered forth in minstrel fashion,
  Underneath the lowering skies;
Sang before each comely Wirthshaus,
  Sang beside each purling stream,
That same ditty which I chanted
  When Undine was my theme,

Singing, as I sang at Jena,
  When the shifts were hung to dry,
"Fair Undine! young Undine!
  Dost thou love as well as I?"

But, alas! in field or village,
  Or beside the pebbly shore,
Did I see those glancing ankles,
  And the white robe nevermore;
And no answer came to greet me,
  No sweet voice to mine replied;
But I heard the waters rippling,
  And the moaning of the tide.

"The moaning of the TIED."

The Lay of the Levite.

THERE is a sound that's dear to me,
  It haunts me in my sleep;
I wake, and, if I hear it not,
  I cannot choose but weep.
Above the roaring of the wind,
  Above the river's flow,
Methinks I hear the mystic cry
  Of " Clo !—Old Clo !"

The exile's song, it thrills among
  The dwellings of the free,
Its sound is strange to English ears,
  But 't is not strange to me;
For it hath shook the tented field
  In ages long ago,
And hosts have quailed before the cry
  Of " Clo !—Old Clo !"

Oh, lose it not! forsake it not!
  And let no time efface
The memory of that solemn sound,
  The watchword of our race.

For not by dark and eagle eye
  The Hebrew shall you know,
So well as by the plaintive cry
  Of "Clo!—Old Clo!"

Even now, perchance, by Jordan's banks,
  Or Sidon's sunny walls,
Where, dial-like, to portion time,
  The palm-tree's shadow falls,
The pilgrims, wending on their way,
  Will linger as they go,
And listen to the distant cry
  Of "Clo!—Old Clo!"

Bursch Groggenburg.

AFTER THE MANNER OF SCHILLER.

"Bursch! if foaming beer content ye,
    Come and drink your fill;
In our cellars there is plenty;
    Himmel! how you swill!
That the liquor hath allurance,
    Well I understand;
But 't is really past endurance,
    When you squeeze my hand!"

And he heard her as if dreaming,
    Heard her half in awe;
And the meerschaum's smoke came streaming
    From his open jaw:
And his pulse beat somewhat quicker
    Than it did before,
And he finished off his liquor,
    Staggered through the door;

Bolted off direct to Munich,
    And within the year
Underneath his German tunic
    Stowed whole butts of beer.
And he drank like fifty fishes,
    Drank till all was blue;
For he felt extremely vicious—
    Somewhat thirsty too.

But at length this dire deboshing
    Drew towards an end;
Few of all his silber-groschen
    Had he left to spend.
And he knew it was not prudent
    Longer to remain;
So, with weary feet, the student
    Wended home again.

At the tavern's well known portal,
    Knocks he as before,
. And a waiter, rather mortal,
    Hiccups through the door,—
" Masters 's sleeping in the kitchen;
    You 'll alarm the house;
Yesterday the Jungfrau Fritchen
    Married baker Kraus!"

Like a fiery comet bristling,
    Rose the young man's hair,
And, poor soul! he fell a-whistling,
    Out of sheer despair.

Down the gloomy street in silence,
    Savage-calm he goes;
But he did no deed of vi'lence—
    Only blew his nose.

Then he hired an airy garret
    Near her dwelling-place;
Grew a beard of fiercest carrot,
    Never washed his face;
Sate all day beside the casement,
    Sate a dreary man;
Found in smoking such an easement
    As the wretched can;

Stared for hours and hours together,
    Stared yet more and more;
Till in fine and sunny weather,
    At the baker's door,
Stood, in apron white and mealy,
    That belovéd dame,
Counting out the loaves so freely,
    Selling of the same.

Then like a volcano puffing,
    Smoked he out his pipe;
Sigh'd and supp'd on ducks and stuffing,
    Ham, and kraut, and tripe;
Went to bed, and in the morning,
    Waited as before,
Still his eyes in anguish turning
    To the baker's door;

Till, with apron white and mealy,
　　Came the lovely dame,
Counting out the loaves so freely,
　　Selling of the same.
So, one day—the fact 's amazing!—
　　On his post he died ;
And they found the body gazing
　　At the baker's bride.

Night and Morning.

NOT BY SIR E. BULWER LYTTON.

"Thy coffee, Tom, 's untasted,
  And thy egg is very cold;
Thy cheeks are wan and wasted,
  Not rosy as of old.
My boy what has come o'er ye,
  You surely are not well!
Try some of that ham before ye,
  And then, Tom, ring the bell!"

"I cannot eat, my mother,
  My tongue is parched and bound,
And my head somehow or other,
  Is swimming round and round.
In my eyes there is a fulness,
  And my pulse is beating quick;
On my brain is a weight of dulness;
  Oh, mother, I am sick!"

" These long, long nights of watching
   Are killing you outright;
The evening dews are catching,
   And you 're out every night.
Why does that horrid grumbler,
   Old Inkpen, work you so ?"

             TOM (*lene susurrans*)

"My head ! Oh, that tenth tumbler !
   'T was that wihch wrought my wo !"

The Biter Bit.

THE sun is in the sky, mother, the flowers are springing
    fair,
And the melody of woodland birds is stirring in the
    air;
The river, smiling to the sky, glides onward to the
    sea,
And happiness is everywhere, oh mother, but with
    me!

They are going to the church, mother,—I hear the
    marriage bell;
It booms along the upland,—oh! it haunts me like a
    knell;
He leads her on his arm, mother, he cheers her faltering
    step,
And closely to his side she clings,—she does, the
    demirep!

They are crossing by the stile, mother, where we so oft
    have stood,
The stile beside the shady thorn, at the corner of the
    wood;

And the boughs, that wont to murmur back the words
    that won my ear,
Wave their silver branches o'er him, as he leads his
    bridal fere.

He will pass beside the stream, mother, where first my
    hand he pressed,
By the meadow where, with quivering lip, his passion
    he confessed;
And down the hedgerows where we 've strayed again
    and yet again;
But he will not think of me, mother, his broken-hearted
    Jane!

He said that I was proud, mother, that I looked for rank
    and gold,
He said I did not love him,—he said my words were
    cold;
He said I kept him off and on, in hopes of higher
    game,—
And it may be that I did, mother; but who has n't done
    the same?

I did not know my heart, mother,—I know it now too
    late;
I thought that I without a pang could wed some nobler
    mate;
But no nobler suitor sought me,—and he has taken
    wing,
And my heart is gone, and I am left a lone and blighted
    thing.

You may lay me in my bed, mother,—my head is
throbbing sore;
And, mother, prithee, let the sheets be duly aired
before;
And, if you 'd please, my mother dear, your poor desponding child,
Draw me a pot of beer, mother, and, mother, draw it
mild!

"Love gone to pot."

The Convict and the Australian Lady.

THY skin is dark as jet, ladye,
  Thy cheek is sharp and high,
And there's a cruel leer, love,
  Within thy rolling eye!
These tangled ebon tresses
  No comb hath e'er gone through;
And thy forehead it is furrowed by
  The elegant tattoo!

I love thee,—oh, I love thee,
  Thou strangely feeding maid!
Nay, lift not thus thy boomerang,
  I meant not to upbraid!
Come, let me taste those yellow lips
  That ne'er were tasted yet,
Save when the shipwrecked mariner
  Pass'd through them for a whet.

Nay, squeeze me not so tightly!
  For I am gaunt and thin,
There's little flesh to tempt thee
  Beneath a convict's skin.

I came not to be eaten,
   I sought thee, love, to woo ;
Besides, bethink thee, dearest,
   Thou 'st dined on cockatoo !

Thy father is a chieftain ;
   Why that's the very thing !
Within my native country
   I, too, have been a king.
Behold this branded letter,
   Which nothing can efface !
It is the royal emblem,
   The token of my race !

But rebels rose against me,
   And dared my power disown—
You've heard, love, of the judges ?
   They drove me from my throne.
And I have wandered hither,
   Across the stormy sea,
In search of glorious freedom,
   In search, my sweet, of thee !

The bush is now my empire,
   The knife my sceptre keen ;
Come with me to the desert wild,
   And be my dusky queen.
I cannot give thee jewels,
   I have nor sheep nor cow,
Yet there are kangaroos, love,
   And colonists enow.

We'll meet the unwary settler,
  As whistling home he goes,
And I'll take tribute from him,
  His money and his clothes.
Then on his bleeding carcass
  Thou'lt lay thy pretty paw,
And lunch upon him roasted,
  Or, if you like it, raw!

Then come with me, my princess,
  My own Australian dear,
Within this grove of gum trees,
  We'll hold our bridal cheer!
Thy heart with love is beating,
  I feel it through my side:—
Hurrah. then, for the noble pair,
  The Convict and his bride!

The Doleful Lay of the Honorable I. O. Uwins.

COME and listen, lords and ladies,
  To a woful lay of mine;
He whose tailor's bill unpaid is,
  Let him now his ear incline!
Let him hearken to my story,
  How the noblest of the land
Pined long time in dreary duresse
  'Neath a sponging bailiff's hand.

I. O. Uwins! I. O. Uwins!
  Baron's son although thou be,
Thou must pay for thy misdoings
  In the country of the free!
None of all thy sire's retainers
  To thy rescue now may come;
And there lie some score detainers,
  With Abednego, the bum.

Little reck'd he of his prison
  Whilst the sun was in the sky:
Only when the moon was risen,
  Did you hear the captive's cry;

For, till then, cigars and claret
    Lull'd him in oblivion sweet;
And he much preferr'd a garret,
    For his drinking, to the street.

But the moonlight, pale and broken,
    Pain'd at soul the Baron's son;
For he knew, by that soft token,
    That the larking had begun;—
That the stout and valiant Marquis
    Then was leading forth his swells,
Mangling some policeman's carcass,
    Or purloining private bells.

So he sat, in grief and sorrow,
    Rather drunk than otherwise,
Till the golden gush of morrow
    Dawned once more upon his eyes:
Till the sponging bailiff's daughter,
    Lightly tapping at the door,
Brought his draught of soda water,
    Brandy-bottom'd as before.

"Sweet Rebecca! has your father,
    Think you, made a deal of brass?"
And she answered—"Sir, I rather
    Should imagine that he has."
Uwins then, his whiskers scratching,
    Leer'd upon the maiden's face,
And, her hand with ardor catching,
    Folded her in close embrace.

"La, Sir! let alone—you fright me!"
    Said the daughter of the Jew:
"Dearest, how those eyes delight me!
    Let me love thee, darling, do!"
"Vat is dish?" the Bailiff mutter'd,
    Rushing in with fury wild;
"Ish your muffins so vell butter'd
    Dat you darsh insult ma shild?"

"Honorable my intentions,
    Good Abednego, I swear!
And I have some small pretensions,
    For I am a Baron's heir.
If you'll only clear my credit,
    And advance a *thou** or so,
She's a peeress—I have said it:
    Don't you twig, Abednego?"

"Datsh a very different matter,"
    Said the Bailiff, with a leer;
"But you musht not cut it fatter
    Than ta slish will shtand, ma tear!
If you seeksh ma approbation,
    You musht quite give up your rigsh;
Alsho you musht join our nashun,
    And renounsh ta flesh of pigsh."

Fast as one of Fagin's pupils,
    I. O. Uwins did agree!
Little plagued with holy scruples
    From the starting post was he.

* The fashionable abbreviation for a thousand pounds

But at times a baleful vision
  Rose before his trembling view,
For he knew that circumcision
  Was expected from a Jew.

At a meeting of the Rabbis
  Held about the Whitsuntide,
Was this thorough-paced Barabbas
  Wedded to his Hebrew bride.
All his former debts compounded,
  From the spunging house he came,
And his father's feelings wounded
  With reflections on the same.

But the sire his son accosted—
  "Split my wig! if any more
Such a double-dyed apostate
  Shall presume to cross my door!
Not a penny-piece to save ye
  From the kennel or the spout;—
Dinner, John! the pig and gravy!—
  Kick this dirty scoundrel out!"

Forth rush'd I. O. Uwins faster
  Than all winking—much afraid,
That the orders of the master
  Would be punctually obeyed:
Sought his club, and then the sentence
  Of expulsion first he saw;
No one dared to own acquaintance
  With a bailiff's son-in-law.

Uselessly down Bond-street strutting
   Did he greet his friends of yore :
Such a universal cutting
   Never man received before :
Till at last his pride revolted—
   Pale, and lean, and stern he grew ;
And his wife Rebecca bolted
   With a missionary Jew.

Ye who read this doleful ditty,
   Ask ye where is Uwins now ?
Wend your way through London city,
   Climb to Holborn's lofty brow.
Near the sign-post of the " Nigger,"
   Near the baked-potato shed,
You may see a ghastly figure
   With three hats upon his head.

When the evening shades are dusky,
   Then the phantom form draws near,
And, with accents low and husky,
   Pours effluvium in your ear :
Craving an immediate barter
   Of your trousers or surtout,
And you know the Hebrew martyr,
   Once the peerless I. O. U.

The Knyghte and the Taylzeour's Daughter.

DID you ever hear the story—
    Old the legend is and true—
How a knyghte of fame and glory
    All aside his armor threw ;
Spouted spear and pawned habergeon,
    Pledged his sword and surcoat gay,
Sate down cross-legged on the shop-board
    Sate and stitched the livelong day ?

"Taylzeour ! not one single shilling
    Does my breeches' pocket hold :
I to pay am really willing,
    If I only had the gold.
Farmers none can I encounter,
    Graziers there are none to kill ;
Therefore, prithee, gentle taylzeour,
    Bother not about thy bill."

" Good Sir Knyghte, just once too often
    Have you tried that slippery trick ;
Hearts like mine you cannot soften,
    Vainly do you ask for tick.

Christmas and its bills are coming,
  Soon will they be showering in;
Therefore, once for all, my rum 'un,
  I expect you 'll post the tin.

"Mark, Sir Knyghte, that gloomy bayliffe,
  In the palmer's amice brown;
He shall lead you unto jail, if
  Instantly you stump not down."
Deeply swore the young crusader,
  But the taylzeour would not hear;
And the gloomy bearded bayliffe
  Evermore kept sneaking near.

"Neither groat nor maravedi
  Have I got my soul to bless;
And I feel extremely seedy,
  Languishing in vile duresse.
Therefore listen, ruthless taylzeour,
  Take my steed and armor free,
Pawn them at thy Hebrew uncle's,
  And I'll work the rest for thee."

Lightly leaped he on the shop-board,
  Lightly crooked his manly limb,
Lightly drove the glancing needle
  Through the growing doublet's rim.
Gaberdines in countless number
  Did the taylzeour-knyghte repair!
And the cabbage and cucumber
  Were his sole and simple fare.

Once his weary task beguiling
   With a low and plaintive song,
That good knyghte o'er miles of broadcloth
   Drove the hissing goose along;
From her lofty lattice window,
   Looked the taylzeour's daughter down,
And she instantly discovered
   That her heart was not her own.

"Canst thou love me, gentle stranger?"
   Blushing like a rose she stood—
And the knyghte at once admitted,
   That he rather thought he could.
"He who weds me shall have riches,
   Gold, and lands, and houses free."
"For a single pair of—*small clothes*,
   I would roam the world with thee!"

Then she flung him down the tickets—
   Well the knyghte their import knew—
"Take this gold, and win thy armor,
   From the unbelieving Jew.
Though in garments mean and lowly,
   Thou wouldst roam the world with me,
Only as a belted warrior,
   Stranger, will I wed with thee!"

At the feast of good Saint Alban,
   In the middle of the Spring,
There was some superior jousting
   By the order of the king.
4*

" Valiant knyghtes !" exclaimed the monarch,
  " You will please to understand,
He who bears himself most bravely,
  Shall obtain my daughter's hand."

Well and bravely did they bear them,
  Bravely battled, one and all ;
But the bravest in the tourney
  Was a warrior stout and tall.
None could tell his name or lineage,
  None could meet him in the field,
And a goose regardant proper
  Hissed along his azure shield.

" Warrior, thou hast won my daughter !"
  But the champion bowed his knee,
" Princely blood may not be wasted
  On a simple knyghte like me.
She I love is meek and lowly ;
  But her heart is high and frank ;
And there must be tin forthcoming,
  That will do as well as rank."

Slowly rose that nameless warrior,
  Slowly turned his steps aside,
Passed the lattice where the princess
  Sate in beauty, sate in pride.
Passed the row of noble ladies,
  Hied him to an humbler seat,
And in silence laid the chaplet
  At the taylzeour's daughter's feet.

The Midnight Visit.

It was the Lord of Castlereagh, he sat within his room,
His arms were crossed upon his breast, his face was
    marked with gloom ;
They said that St. Helena's Isle had rendered up its
    charge,
That France was bristling high in arms,—the Emperor
    at large.

'Twas midnight! all the lamps were dim, and dull as
    death the street,
It might be that the watchman slept that night upon his
    beat,
When, lo! a heavy foot was heard to creak upon the
    stair,
The door revolved upon its hinge,—Great Heaven!—
    What enters there?

A little man, of stately mien, with slow and solemn
    stride ;
His hands are crossed upon his back, his coat is opened
    wide :

And on his vest of green he wears an eagle and a
    star,—
Saint George! protect us! 't is THE MAN—the thunder-
    bolt of war!

Is that the famous hat that waved along Marengo's
    ridge?
Are these the spurs of Austerlitz—the boots of Lodi's
    bridge?
Leads he the conscript swarm again from France's hornet
    hive?
What seeks the fell usurper here, in Britain, and alive?

Pale grew the Lord of Castlereagh, his tongue was
    parched and dry,
As in his brain he felt the glare of that tremendous eye;
What wonder if he shrunk in fear, for who could meet
    the glance
Of him who reared, 'mid Russian snows, the gonfalon
    of France?

From the side-pocket of his vest, a pinch the despot
    took,
Yet not a whit did he relax the sternness of his look,—
"Thou thought'st the lion was afar, but he hath burst
    the chain—
The watchword for to-night is France—the answer, St.
    Heléne.

" And didst thou deem the barren isle, or ocean waves,
    could bind
The master of the universe—the monarch of mankind?

I tell thee, fool! the world itself is all too small for me,
I laugh to scorn thy bolts and bars—I burst them, and
am free.

"Thou think'st that England hates me! Mark!—This
very night my name
Was thundered in its capital with tumult and acclaim!
They saw me, knew me, owned my power—Proud lord!
I say, beware!
There be men within the Surrey side, who know to do
and dare!

"To-morrow, in thy very teeth, my standard will I rear—
Ay, well that ashen cheek of thine may blanch and
shrink with fear!
To-morrow night another town shall sink in ghastly
flames;
And as I crossed the Borodin, so shall I cross the
Thames!

"Thou 'lt seize me, wilt thou, ere the dawn? Weak
lordling, do thy worst?
These hands ere now have broke thy chains, thy fetters
they have burst.
Yet, wouldst thou know my resting-place? Behold 't is
written there!
And let thy coward myrmidons approach me if they
dare!"

Another pinch, another stride—he passes through the
door—
" Was it a phantom or a man was standing on the floor?

And could that be the Emperor that moved before my
    eyes?
Ah, yes! too sure it was himself, for here the paper
    lies!"

With trembling hands, Lord Castlereagh undid the mys-
    tic scroll,
With glassy eye essayed to read, for fear was on his
    soul—
What's here?—'At Astley's, every night, the play of
    Moscow's FALL!
NAPOLEON for the thousandth time, by Mr. GOMERSAL!"

The Lay of the Lovelorn.

COMRADES, you may pass the rosy. With permission
of the chair,
I shall leave you for a little, for I'd like to take the air.

Whether 't was the sauce at dinner, or that glass of ginger beer,
Or these strong cheroots, I know not, but I feel a little
queer.

Let me go. Now, Chuckster, blow me, 'pon my soul,
this is too bad!
When you want me, ask the waiter, he knows where
I'm to be had.

Whew! This is a great relief now! Let me but undo
my stock,
Resting here beneath the porch, my nerves will steady
like a rock.

In my ears I hear the singing of a lot of favorite tunes—
Bless my heart, how very odd! Why, surely there's a
brace of moons!

See ! the stars ! how bright they twinkle, winking with
    a frosty glare,
Like my faithless cousin Amy when she drove me to
    despair.

O, my cousin, spider-hearted ! Oh, my Amy ! No,
    confound it !
I must wear the mournful willow,—all around my hat
    I've bound it.

Falser than the Bank of Fancy,—frailer than a shilling
    glove,
Puppet to a father's anger,—minion to a nabob's love !

Is it well to wish thee happy ? Having known me,
    could you ever
Stoop to marry half a heart, and little more than half a
    liver ?

Happy ! Damme ! Thou shalt lower to his level day
    by day,
Changing from the best of China to the commonest of
    clay.

As the husband is, the wife is,—he is stomach-plagued
    and old ;
And his curry soups will make thy cheek the color of
    his gold.

When his feeble love is sated, he will hold thee surely
    then
Something lower than his hookah,—something less than
    his cayenne.

What is this? His eyes are pinky. Was't the claret?
  Oh, no, no,—
Bless your soul, it was the salmon,—salmon always
  makes him so.

Take him to thy dainty chamber—soothe him with thy
  lightest fancies,
He will understand thee, won't he?—pay thee with a
  lover's glances?

Louder than the loudest trumpet, harsh as harshest
  ophicleide,
Nasal respirations answer the endearments of his bride.

Sweet response, delightful music! Gaze upon thy noble
  charge
Till the spirit fill thy bosom that inspired the meek
  Laffarge.

Better thou wert dead before me,—better, better that I
  stood
Looking on thy murdered body, like the injured Daniel
  Good!

Better, thou and I were lying, cold and timber-stiff and
  dead,
With a pan of burning charcoal underneath our nuptial
  bed!

Cursed be the bank of England's notes, that tempt the
  soul to sin!
Cursed be the want of acres,—doubly cursed the want
  of tin!

Cursed be the marriage contract, that enslaved thy soul
to greed!
Cursed be the sallow lawyer, that prepared and drew
the deed!

Cursed be his foul apprentice, who the loathsome fees
did earn!
Cursed be the clerk and parson,—cursed be the whole
concern!

    *   *   *   *

Oh, 't is well that I should bluster,—much I'm like to
make of that;
Better comfort have I found in singing " All Around my
Hat."

But that song, so wildly plaintive, palls upon my British
ears.
'T will not do to pine for ever,—I am getting up in
years.

Can't I turn the honest penny, scribbling for the weekly
press,
And in writing Sunday libels drown my private wretch-
edness?

Oh, to feel the wild pulsation that in manhood's dawn I
knew,
When my days were all before me, and my years were
twenty-two.

THE BOOK OF BALLADS. 91

When I smoked my independent pipe along the Quad-
rant wide,
With the many larks of London flaring up on every
side.

When I went the pace so wildly, caring little what might
come,
Coffee-milling care and sorrow, with a nose-adapted
thumb.

Felt the exquisite enjoyment, tossing nightly off, oh
heavens!
Brandy at the Cider Cellars, kidneys smoking-hot at
Evans'!

Or in the Adelphi sitting, half in rapture, half in tears,
Saw the glorious melo-drama conjure up the shades of
years!

Saw Jack Sheppard, noble stripling, act his wondrous
feats again,
Snapping Newgate's bars of iron, like an infant's daisy
chain.

Might was right, and all the terrors which had held the
world in awe
Were despised, and prigging prospered, spite of Laurie,
spite of law.

In such scenes as these I triumphed, ere my passion's
edge was rusted,
And my cousin's cold refusal left me very much disgusted!

Since, my heart is sere and withered, and I do not care
    a curse
Whether worse shall be the better, or the better be the
    worse.

Hark! my merry comrades call me, bawling for another
    jorum;
They would mock me in derision, should I thus appear
    before 'em.

Womankind no more shall vex me, such at least, as go
    arrayed
In the most expensive satins, and the newest silk brocade.

I 'll to Afric, lion-haunted, where the giant forest yields
Rarer robes and finer tissue than are sold at Spital
    fields.

Or to burst all chains of habit, flinging habit's self
    aside,
I shall walk the tangled jungle in mankind's primeval
    pride;

Feeding on the luscious berries and the rich cassava
    root,
Lots of dates and lots of guavas, clusters of forbidden
    fruit.

Never comes the trader thither, never o'er the purple
    main
Sounds the oath of British commerce, or the accents of
    Cockaigne.

There, methinks, would be enjoyment, where no envirous
    rule prevents;
Sink the steamboats! cuss the railways! rot, O rot the
    Three per Cents!

There the passions, cramped no longer, shall have space
    to breathe, my cousin!
I will take some savage woman—nay, I 'll take at least
    a dozen.

There I 'll rear my young mulattoes, as no Bond Street
    brats are reared:
They shall dive for aligators, catch the wild goats by the
    beard—

Whistle to the cockatoos, and mock the hairy-faced
    baboon,
Worship mighty Mumbo Jumbo in the Mountains of
    the Moon.

I myself, in far Timbuctoo, leopard's blood will daily
    quaff,
Ride a tiger-hunting, mounted on a thorough-bred giraffe.

Fiercely shall I shout the war-whoop, as some sullen
    stream he crosses,
Startling from their noon-day slumbers, iron-bound rhino-
    ceroses.

Fool! again the dream, the fancy! But I know my
    words are mad,
For I hold the grey barbarian lower than the Christian
    cad.

I the swell—the city dandy! I to seek such horrid
    places,—
I to haunt with squalid negroes, blubber-lips, and mon-
    key faces.

I to wed with Coromantees! I, who managed—very
    near—
To secure the heart and fortune of the widow Shilli-
    beer !

Stuff and nonsense! let me never fling a single chance
    away,
Maids ere now, I know, have loved me, and another
    maiden may.

" Morning Post," ("The Times" won't trust me) help
    me, as I know you can;
I will pen an advertisement,—that 's a never-failing
    plan.

" WANTED—By a bard in wedlock, some young inter-
    esting woman :
Looks are not so much an object, if the shiners be forth-
    coming !

" Hymen's chains, the advertiser vows, shall be but silken
    fetters,
Please address to A. T., Chelsea.   N. B.—You must pay
    the letters."

That 's the sort of thing to do it.   Now I 'll go and
    taste the balmy,—
Rest thee with thy yellow nabob, spider-hearted cousin
    Amy !

My Wife's Cousin.

DECKED with shoes of blackest polish,
  And with shirt as white as snow,
After matutinal breakfast
  To my daily desk I go;
First a fond salute bestowing
  On my Mary's ruby lips,
Which, perchance, may be rewarded
  With a pair of playful nips.

All day long across the ledger
  Still my patient pen I drive,
Thinking what a feast awaits me
  In my happy home at five;
In my small, one-storied Eden,
  Where my wife awaits my coming,
And our solitary handmaid
  Mutton chops with care is crumbing.

When the clock proclaims my freedom,
  Then my hat I seize and vanish;
Every trouble from my bosom,
  Every anxious care I banish.

Swiftly brushing o'er the pavement,
    At a furious pace I go,
Till I reach my darling dwelling
    In the wilds of Pimlico.

"Mary, wife, where art thou, dearest?"
    Thus I cry, while yet afar;
Ah! what scent invades my nostrils?—
    'T is the smoke of a cigar!
Instantly into the parlor
    Like a maniac I haste,
And I find a young Life-Guardsman,
    With his arm round Mary's waist.

And his other hand is playing
    Most familiarly with hers;
And I think my Brussels carpet
    Somewhat damaged by his spurs.
"Fire and furies! what the blazes?"
    Thus in frenzied wrath I call;
When my spouse her arms upraises,
    With a most astounding squall.

" Was there ever such a monster:
    Ever such a wretched wife?
Ah! how long must I endure it:
    How protract this hateful life?
All day long quite unprotected,
    Does he leave his wife at home;
And she cannot see her cousins,
    Even when they kindly come!"

Then the young Life-Guardsman, rising,
  Scarce vouchsafes a single word,
But with look of deadly menace,
  Claps his hand upon his sword;
And in fear I faintly falter—
  "This your cousin, then he 's mine!
Very glad, indeed, to see you,—
  Won't you stop with us, and dine?"

Won't a ferret suck a rabbit ?—
  As a thing of course he stops ;
And, with most voracious swallow
  Walks into my mutton chops.
In the twinkling of a bed-post,
  Is each savoury platter clear,
And he shows uncommon science
  In his estimate of beer.

Half-and-half goes down before him,
  Gurgling from the pewter-pot ;
And he moves a counter motion
  For a glass of something hot.
Neither chops nor beer I grudge him,
  Nor a moderate share of goes ;
But I know not why he's always
  Treading upon Mary's toes.

Evermore, when home returning,
  From the counting house I come,
Do I find the young Life-Guardsman
  Smoking pipes and drinking rum.
5

Evermore he stays to dinner,
　Evermore devours my meal ;
For I have a wholesome horror
　Both of powder and of steel.

Yet I know he 's Mary's cousin,
　For my only son and heir
Much resembles that young Guardsman,
　With the self-same curly hair ·
But I wish he would not always
　Spoil my carpet with his spurs ;
And I 'd rather see his fingers
　In the fire, than touching hers.

The Queen in France.

AN ANCIENT SCOTTISH BALLAD.

PART I.

It fell upon the August month,
 When landsmen bide at hame,
That our gude Queen went out to sail
 Upon the saut-sea faem.

And she has ta'en the silk and gowd,
 The like was never seen;
And she has ta'en the Prince Albert,
 And the bauld Lord Aberdeen.

"Ye'se bide at hame, Lord Wellington:
 Ye daurna gang wi' me:
For ye hae been ance in the land o' France
 And that's eneuch for ye."

"Ye'se bide at hame, Sir Robert Peel,
To gather the red and the white monie;
 And see that my men dinna eat me up
At Windsor wi' their gluttonie."

They hadna sailed a league, a league,—
  A league, but barely twa,
When the lift grew dark, and the waves grew wan,
  And the wind began to blaw.

" O weel, weel may the waters rise,
  In welcome o' their Queen ;
What gars ye look sae white, Albert ?
  What makes your e'e sae green ?"

"My heart is sick, my heid is sair:
  Gie me a glass o' gude brandie :
To set my foot on the braid green sward.
  I 'd gie the half o' my yearly fee.

" It 's sweet to hunt the sprightly hare
  On the bonny slopes o' Windsor lea,
But O, it 's ill to bear the thud
  And pitching o' the saut, saut sea !"

And aye they sailed, and aye they sailed,
  Till England sank behind,
And over to the coast of France
  They drave before the wind.

Then up and spak the King o' France,
  Was birling at the wine ;
" O wha may be the gay ladye
  That owns that ship sae fine ?

" And wha may be that bonny lad,
  That looks sae pale and wan ?
I 'll wad my lands o' Picardie
  That he 's nae Englishman."

Then up and spak an auld French lord,
  Was sitting beneath his knee,
" It is the Queen o' braid England
  That's come across the sea."

" And O an it be England's Queen,
  She's welcome here the day ;
I 'd rather hae her for a friend
  Than for a deadly fae.

" Gae, kill the cerock in the yard,
  The auld sow in the stye,
And bake for her the brockit calf,
  But and the puddock-pie !"

And he has gane until the ship,
  As sune as it drew near,
And he has ta'en her by the hand—
  " Ye 're kindly welcome here !"

And syne he kissed her on ae cheek,
  And syne upon the ither ;
And he ca'ed her his sister dear,
  And she ca'ed him her brither.

" Light doun, light doun now, layde mine,
  Light doun upon the shore ;
Nae English king has trodden here,
  This thousand years and more."

" And gin I lighted on your land,
  As light fu' weel I may,
O am I free to feast wi' you,
  And free to come and gae ?"

And he has sworn by the Haly Rood,
　And the black staue o' Dumblane,
That she is free to come and gae
　Till twenty days are gane.

"I 've lippened to a Frenchman's aith,"
　Said gude Lord Aberdeen;
"But I 'll never lippen to it again
　Sae lang 's the grass is green.

"Yet gae your ways, my sovereign liege,
　Since better may na be;
The wee bit bairns are safe at hame,
　By the blessing o' Marie!"

Then doun she lighted frae the ship,
　She lighted safe and sound;
And glad was our good Prince Albert
　To step upon the ground.

"Is that your Queen, My Lord," she said,
　"That auld and buirdly dame?
I see the crown upon her heid;
　But I dinna ken her name."

And she has kissed the Frenchman's Queen,
　And eke her daughters three,
And gi'en her hand to the young Princess
　That louted upon the knee.

And she has gane to the proud castle,
　That 's biggit beside the sea:
But aye, when she thought o' the bairns at hame,
　The tear was in her e'e.

She gied the King the Cheshire cheese,
    But and the porter fine;
And he gied her the puddock-pies,
    But and the blude-red wine.

Then up and spak the dourest prince,
    An Admiral was he;
"Let 's keep the Queen o' England here,
    Sin' better may na be!

"O mony is the dainty king
    That we hae trappit here;
And mony is the English yerl
    That 's in our dungeons drear!"

"You lee, you lee, ye graceless loon,
    Sae loud 's I hear ye lee!
There never yet was Englishman
    That came to skaith by me.

"Gae out, gae out, ye fause traitor!
    Gae out until the street;
It 's shame that Kings and Queens should sit
    Wi' sic a knave at meat!"

Then up and raise the young French lord,
    In wrath and hie disdain—
"O ye may sit, and ye may eat
    Your puddock-pies alane!

"But were I in my ain gude ship,
    And sailing wi' the wind,
And did I meet wi' auld Napier,
    I 'd tell him o' my mind."

O then the Queen leuch loud and lang,
    And her color went and came;
"Gin ye met wi' Charlie on the sea
    Ye 'd wish yersell at hame !"

And aye they birlit at the wine,
    And drank right merrilie,
Till the auld cock crawed in the castle-yard,
    And the abbey bell struck three.

The Queen she gaed until her bed,
    And Prince Albert likewise ;
And the last word that gay ladye said
    Was—" O thae puddock-pies !"

PART II.

The sun was high within the lift
    Afore the French King raise ;
And syne he louped intil his sark,
    And warslit on his claes.

" Gae up, gae up, my little foot-page,
    Gae up until the toun ;
And gin ye meet wi' the auld harper,
    Be sure ye bring him doun."

And he has met wi' the auld harper;
    O but his e'en were red ;
And the bizzing o' a swarm o' bees
    Was singing in his heid.

"Alack! alack!" the harper said,
"That this should e'er hae been!
I daurna gang before my liege,
For I was fou yestreen."

"It 's ye maun come, ye auld harper:
Ye daurna tarry lang;
The King is just dementit-like
For wanting o' a sang."

And when he came to the King's chamber,
He loutit on his knee,
"O what may be your gracious will
Wi' an auld frail man like me?"

"I want a sang, harper," he said,
"I want a sang richt speedilie;
And gin ye dinna make a sang,
I 'll hang ye up on the gallows-tree."

"I cannot do.'t, my liege," he said,
"Hae mercy on my auld gray hair!
But gin that I had got the words,
I think that I might mak the air."

"And wha 's to mak the words, fause loon,
When minstrels we have barely twa;
And Lamartine is in Paris toun,
And Victor Hugo far awa?"

"The deil may gang for Lamartine,
And flie awa wi' auld Hugo,
For a better minstrel than them baith
Within this very toun I know.
5*

"O kens my liege the gude Walter,—
   At hame they ca' him BON GAULTIER?
He 'll rhyme ony day wi' True Thomas,
   And he is in the castle here."

The French King first he lauchit loud,
   And syne did he begin to sing;
"My e'en are auld, and my heart is cauld,
   Or I suld hae known the minstrels' King.

"Gae take to him this ring o' gowd,
   And this mantle o' the silk sae fine,.
And bid him mak a maister sang
   For his sovereign ladye's sake and mine."

"I winna take the gowden ring,
   Nor yet the mantle fine:
But I'll mak the sang for my ladye's sake,
   And for a cup of wine."

The Queen was sitting at the cards,
   The King ahint her back;
And aye she dealed the red honors,
   And aye she dealed the black;

And syne unto the dourest Prince
   She spak richt courteouslie :—
"Now will ye play, Lord Admiral,
   Now will ye play wi' me?"

The dourest prince he bit his lip,
   And his brow was black as glaur :
"The only game that e'er I play
   Is the bluidy game o' war!"

"And gin ye play at that, young man,
    It weel may cost ye sair ;
Ye 'd better stick to the game at cards,
    For you 'll win nae honors there !"

The King he leuch, and the Queen she leuch,
    Till the tears ran blithely doun ;
But the Admiral he raved and swore,
    Till they kicked him frae the room.

The Harper came, and the Harper sang,
    And O but they were fain ;
For when he had sung the gude sang twice,
    They called for it again.

It was the sang o' the Field o' Gowd,
    In the days of auld lang syne ;
When bauld King Henry crossed the seas,
    Wi' his brither King to dine.

And aye he harped, and aye he carped,
    Till up the Queen she sprang—
"I 'll wad a County Palatine,
    Gude Walter made that sang."

Three days had come, three days had gane,
    The fourth began to fa',
When our gude Queen to the Frenchman.said,
    "It 's time I was awa !

"O, bonny are the fields o' France,
    And saftly draps the rain ;
But my bairnies are in Windsor Tower,
    And greeting a' their lane.

" Now ye maun come to me, Sir King,
　　As I have come to ye;
And a benison upon your heid
　　For a' your courtesie!

"Ye maun come, and bring your ladye fere:
　　Ye sall na say me no;
And ye 'se mind, we have aye a bed to spare
　　For your wily friend Guizot."

Now he has ta'en her lily white hand,
　　And put it to his lip,
And he has ta'en her to the strand,
　　And left her in her ship.

" Will ye come back, sweet bird," he cried,
　　"Will ye come kindly here,
When the lift is blue, and the lavrocks sing,
　　In the spring-time o' the year?"

"It 's I would blithely come, my Lord,
　　To see ye in the spring;
It 's I would blithely venture back,
　　But for ae little thing.

"It is na that the winds are rude,
　　Or that the waters rise,
But I lo'e the roasted beef at hame,
　　And no thae puddock-pies!"

The Massacre of the Macpherson.

FROM THE GAELIC.

I.

FHAIRSTON swore a feud
  Against the clan M'Tavish;
Marched into their land
  To murder and to rafish:
For he did resolve
  To extirpate the vipers,
With four and-twenty men,
  And five-and-thirty pipers.

II.

But when he had gone
  Half-way down Strath Canaan,
Of his fighting tail
  Just three were remainin'.
They were all he had,
  To back him in ta battle;
All the rest had gone
  Off, to drive ta cattle.

III.

"Fery coot!" cried Fhairshon,
　"So my clan disgraced is;
Lads, we 'll need to fight
　Pefore we touch the peasties.
Here 's Mhic-Mac-Methusalen
　Coming wi' his fassals,
Gillies seventy-three,
　And sixty Dhuinéwassails!"

IV.

"Coot tay to you, sir;
　Are not you ta Fhairshon?
Was you coming here
　To visit any person?
You are a plackguard, sir!
　It is now six hundred
Coot long years, and more,
　Since my glen was plundered."

V.

Fat is tat you say?
　Dar you cock your peaver?
I will teach you, sir,
　Fat is coot pehavior!
You shall not exist
　For another day more;
I will shot you, sir,
　Or stap you with my claymore!"

VI.

"I am fery glad
  To learn what you mention,
Since I can prevent
  Any such intention."
So Mhic-Mac-Methusaleh
  Gave some warlike howls,
Trew his skhian-dhu,
  An' stuck it in his powels.

VII.

In this fery way
  Tied ta faliant Fhairshon,
Who was always thought
  A superior person.
Fhairshon had a son,
  Who married Noah's daughter,
And nearly spoiled ta Flood,
  By trinking up ta water.

VIII.

Which he would have done,
  I at least believe it,
Had ta mixture peen
  Only half Glenlivet.
This is all my tale:
  Sirs, I hope 't is new t' ye!
Here 's your fery good healths,
  And tamn ta whusky tuty!

The Young Stockbroker's Bride.

"O SWIFTLY speed the gallant bark !—
  I say, you mind my luggage, porter !
I do not heed yon storm-cloud dark,
  I go to wed old Jenkin's daughter.
I go to claim my own Mariar,
  The fairest flower that blooms in Harwich ;
My panting bosom is on fire,
  And all is ready for the marriage."

Thus spoke young Mivins, as he stepped
  On board the "Firefly," Harwich packet ;
The bell rung out, the paddles swept
  Plish-plashing round with noisy racket.
The lowering clouds young Mivins saw,
  But fear, he felt, was only folly ;
And so he smoked a fresh cigar,
  Then fell to whistling—"Nix my dolly !"

The wind it roared ; the packet's hulk
  Rocked with a most unpleasant motion ;
Young Mivins leant him o'er a bulk,
  And poured his sorrows to the ocean.

Tints—blue and yellow—signs of wo—
   Flushed, rainbow-like, his noble face in,
As suddenly he rushed below,
   Crying, "Steward, steward, bring a basin!"

On sped the bark : the howling storm
   The funnel's tapering smoke did blow far ;
Unmoved, young Mivins' lifeless form
   Was stretched upon a hair-cloth sofar.
All night he moaned, the steamer groaned,
   And he was hourly getting fainter ;
When it came bump against the pier,
   And there was fastened by the painter.

Young Mivins rose, and blew his nose,
   Caught wildly at his small portmanteau ;
He was unfit to lie or sit,
   And found it difficult to stand, too.
He sought the deck, he sought the shore,
   He sought the lady's house like winking,
And asked, low tapping at the door,
   "Is this the house of Mr. Jenkin?"

A short man came—he told his name—
   Mivins was short—he cut him shorter,
For in a fury, he exclaimed,
   "Are you the man as vants my darter?
Vot kim'd on you last night, young squire?"
   "It was the steamer, rot and scuttle her!"
"Mayhap it vos, but our Mariar,
   Valked off last night vith Bill the butler.

"And so you 've kim'd a post too late."
" It was the packet, sir, miscarried!"
"Vy, does you think a gal can vait
    As sets 'er 'art on being married?
Last night she vowed she 'd be a bride,
    And 'ave a spouse for vuss or better :
So Bill struck in; the knot vos tied,
    And now I vishes you may get her!"

Young Mivins turned him from the spot,
    Bewilder'd with the dreadful stroke, her
Perfidy came like a shot—
    He was a thunderstruck stockbroker.
"A curse on steam and steamers too!
    By their delays I 've been undone!"
He cried, as, looking very blue,
    He rode a bachelor to London.

The Laureates' Tourney.

BY THE HON. T—— B—— M'A——.

[THIS and the five following poems were among those forwarded to
the Home Secretary, by the unsuccessful competitors for the Laureate-
ship, on its becoming vacant by the death of Southey. How they
came in our possession is a matter between Sir James Graham and
ourselves. The result of the contest could never have been doubtful,
least of all the great poet who then succeeded to the bays. His own
sonnet on the subject, is full of the serene consciousness of superiority,
which does not even admit the idea of rivalry, far less of defeat.

Bays, which in former days have graced the brow
   Of some, who lived and loved, and sung and died;
   Leaves, that were gathered on the pleasant side
Of old Parnassus from Apollo's bough;
With palpitating hand I take ye now,
   Since worthier minstrel there is none beside,
   And with a thrill of song half deified,
I bind them proudly on my locks of snow,
There shall they bide, till he who follows next,
   Of whom I cannot even guess the name,
Shall by Court favor, or some vain pretext
   Of fancied merit, desecrate the same,—
And think, perchance, he wears them quite as well
As the sole bard who sang of Peter Bell!]

FYTTE THE FIRST.

" WHAT news, what news, thou pilgrim grey, what news
    from southern land ?
How fare the bold Conservatives, how is it with Ferrand ?

How does the little Prince of Wales—how looks our
    lady Queen ;
And tell me, is the gentle Brough* once more at Windsor
    seen ?"

" I bring no tidings from the court, nor from St. Stephen's
    hall ;
I 've heard the thundering tramp of horse, and the
    trumpet's battle call ;
And these old eyes have seen a fight, which England
    ne'er hath seen,
Since fell King Richard sobbed his soul through blood
    on Bosworth Green.

" He 's dead, he 's dead, the Laureate's dead !" 'Twas
    thus the cry began,
And straightway every garret roof gave up its minstrel
    man ;
From Grub Street, and from Houndsditch, and from
    Farringdon Within,
The poets all towards Whitehall poured on with eldritch
    din.

Loud yelled they for Sir James the Graham : but sore
    afraid was he ;
A hardy knight were he that might face such a min-
    strelsie.

---

* For the convenience of future commentators it may be mentioned, that the
"gentle Brough" was the Monthly Nurse who attended her Majesty on the
occasion of the birth of the Princess Royal.

"Now by St. Giles of Netherby, my 'patron saint, I
    swear,
I 'd rather by a thousand crowns Lord Palmerston were
    here!—

"What is 't ye seek, ye rebel knaves, what make you
    there beneath?"
"The bays, the bays! we want the bays! we seek the
    laureate wreath!
We seek the butt of generous wine that cheers the sons
    of song:
Choose thou among us all, Sir Knight—we may not
    tarry long!"

Loud laughed the good Sir James in scorn—"Rare jest
    it were, I think,
But one poor butt of Xeres, and a thousand rogues to
    drink!
An' if it flowed with wine or beer, 't is easy to be seen
That dry within the hour would be the well of Hippo-
    crene.

"Tell me, if on Parnassus' heights there grow a thou-
    sand sheaves:
Or has Apollo's laurel bush yet borne ten hundred
    leaves?
Or if so many leaves were there, how long would they
    sustain
The ravage and the glutton bite of such a locust
    train?

"No! get ye back into your dens, take counsel for the
    night,
And choose me out two champions to meet in deadly
    fight;
To-morrow's dawn shall see the lists marked out in
    Spitalfields,
And he who wins shall have the bays, and he shall die
    who yields!"

Down went the window with a crash,—in silence and in
    fear
Each ragged bard looked anxiously upon his neighbor
    near;
Then up and spake young Tennyson—"Who's here that
    fears for death?
'T were better one of us should die, than England lose
    the wreath!

"Let's cast the lots among us now, which two shall fight
    to-morrow;—
For armor bright we 'll club our mite, and horses we
    can borrow.
'T were shame that bards of France should sneer, and
    German *Dichters* too,
If none of British song might dare a deed of *derring-do!*"

"The lists of love are mine," said Moore, "and not the
    lists of Mars;"
Said Hunt, "I seek the jars of wine, but shun the com
    bat's jars!"

"I 'm old," quoth Samuel Rogers.—"Faith," says
Campbell, "so am I!"
"And I 'm in holy orders, sir!" quoth Tom of Ingoldsby.

"Now out upon ye, craven loons!" cried Moxon, good
at need,—
"Bide, if ye will, secure at home, and sleep while others
bleed.
I second Alfred's motion, boys,—let 's try the chance of
lot;
And monks shall sing, and bells shall ring, for him that
goes to pot."

Eight hundred minstrels slunk away—two hundred
stayed to draw,—
Now heaven protect the daring wight that pulls the
longest straw!
'T is done! 't is done! And who hath won? Keep
silence, one and all,—
The first is William Wordsworth hight, the second Ned
Fitzball!"

FYTTE THE SECOND.

OH, bright and gay hath dawned the day on lordly
Spitalfields,—
How flash the rays with ardent blaze from polished
helms and shields!
On either side the chivalry of England throng the
green,
And in the middle balcony appears our gracious Queen.

With iron fists, to keep the lists, two valiant knights
    appear,
The Marquis Hal of Waterford, and stout Sir Aubrey
    Vere.
"What ho, there, herald, blow the trump! Let's see
    who comes to claim
The butt of golden Xeres, and the Laureate's honored
    name!"

That instant dashed into the lists, all armed from head
    to heel,
On courser brown, with vizor down, a warrior sheathed
    in steel;
Then said our Queen—"Was ever seen so stout a knight
    and tall?
His name—his race?"—"An't please your grace, it is
    the brave Fitzball.

"Oft in the Melodrama line his prowess hath been
    shown,
And well throughout the Surrey side his thirst for blood
    is known.
But see, the other champion comes!"—Then rung the
    startled air
With shouts of "Wordsworth, Wordsworth, ho! the
    bard of Rydal's there."

And lo! upon a little steed, unmeet for such a
    course,
Appeared the honored veteran; but weak seemed man
    and horse.

Then shook their ears the sapient peers,—"That joust
 will soon be done:
My Lord of Brougham, I 'll back Fitzball, and give you
 two to one!"

"Done," quoth the Brougham,—"and done with you!"
"Now, Minstrels, are you ready ?"
Exclaimed the Lord of Waterford,—"You 'd better
 both sit steady.
Blow, trumpets, blow the note of charge! and forward
 to the fight!"
"Amen!" said good Sir Aubrey Vere; "Saint Schism
 defend the right!"

As sweeps the blast against the mast, when blows the
 furious squall,
So started at the trumpet's sound, the terrible Fitzball ;
His lance he bore his breast before,—Saint George protect the just,
Or Wordsworth's hoary head must roll along the shame-
 ful dust!

"Who threw that calthrop? Seize the knave!" Alas
 the deed is done;
Down went the steed, and o'er his head flew bright
 Apollo's son.
"Undo his helmet! cut the lace! pour water on his
 head!"
"It ain't no use at all, my lord; 'cos vy? the covey 's
 dead!"

6

Above him stood the Rydal bard—his face was full of
    wo—
" Now there thou liest, stiff and stark, who never feared
    a foe :
A braver knight, or more renowned in tourney and in
    hall,
Ne'er brought the upper gallery down, than terrible
    Fitzball !"

They led our Wordsworth to the Queen—she crowned
    him with the bays,
And wished him many happy years, and many quarter-
    days,—
And if you 'd have the story told by abler lips than
    mine,
You 've but to call at Rydal Mount, and taste the
    Laureate's wine !

The Royal Banquet.

BY THE HON. G———— S———— S————.

THE Queen, she kept high festival in Windsor's lordly
    hall,
And round her sat the gartered knights, and ermined
    nobles all ;
There drank the valiant Wellington, there fed the wary
    Peel,
And at the bottom of the board, Prince Albert carved
    the veal.

" What, pantler, ho ! remove the cloth !   Ho ! cellarer,
    the wine,
And bid the royal nurse bring in the hope of Brunswick's
    line !"
Then rose, with one tumultuous shout, the band of
    British peers,
" God bless her sacred Majesty !   Let 's see the little
    dears !"

Now by Saint George, our patron saint, 't was a touching sight to see
That iron warrior gently place the Princess on his
  knee;
To hear him hush her infant fears, and teach her how to
  gape
With rosy mouth expectant for the raisin and the
  grape!

They passed the wine, the sparkling wine—they filled
  the goblets up,
Even Brougham, the cynic anchorite, smiled blandly on
  the cup;
And Lyndhurst, with a noble thirst, that nothing could
  appease,
Proposed the immortal memory of King William on his
  knees.

"What want we here, my gracious liege," cried good
  Lord Aberdeen,.
"Save gladsome song and minstrelsy to flow our cups
  between?
I ask not now for Goulburn's voice or Knatchbull's
  warbling lay,
But where's the Poet Laureate to grace our board to-
  day?"

Loud laughed the Knight of Netherby, and scornfully he
  cried,
"Or art thou mad with wine, Lord Earl, or art thyself
  beside?

Eight hundred Bedlam bards have claimed the Laureate's
vacant crown,
And now like frantic Bacchanals run wild through London town!"

"Now glory to our gracious Queen!" a voice was heard
to cry,
And dark Macaulay stood before them all with frenzied
eye;
"Now glory to our gracious Queen, and all her glorious
race,
A boon, a boon, my sovran liege! Give me the Laureate's place!

" 'T was I that sang the might of Rome, the glories of
Navarre;
And who could swell the fame so well of Britain's Isles
afar?
The hero of a hundred fights—" Then Wellington up
sprung,
"Ho, silence in the ranks, I say! Sit down, and hold
your tongue.

" By heaven thou shalt not twist my name into a jingling
lay,
Or mimic in thy puny song the thunders of Assaye!
'T is hard that for thy lust of place in peace we cannot
dine.
Nurse, take her Royal Highness here! Sir Robet, pass
the wine!"

"No laureate need we at our board!" then spoke the
    Lord of Vaux ;
"Here 's many a voice to charm the ear with minstrel
    song, I know.
Even I, myself—" Then rose the cry—" A song, a song
    from Brougham !"
He sang,—and straightway found himself alone within
    the room.

The Bard of Erin's Lament.

BY T—— M—RE, ESQ.

OH, weep for the hours when the little blind boy
  Wove round me the spells of his Paphian bower;
When I dipp'd my light wings in the nectar of joy,
  And soar'd in the sunshine, the moth of the hour!
From beauty to beauty, I pass'd like the wind;
  Now fondled the lily, now toy'd with the rose;
And the fair, that at morn had enchanted my mind,
  Was forsook for another ere evening's close.

I sighed not for honor, I cared not for fame,
  While Pleasure sat by me, and Love was my guest;
They twined a fresh wreath for each day as it came,
  And the bosom of beauty still pillowed my rest;
And the harp of my country—neglected it slept—
  In hall or by greenwood unheard were its songs;
From Love's Sybarite dreams I aroused me, and swept
  Its chord to the tale of her glories and wrongs.

But weep for the hour!—Life's summer is past,
   And the snow of its winter lies cold on my brow;
And my soul, as it shrinks from each stroke of the blast,
   Cannot turn to a fire that glows inwardly now.
No, its ashes are dead—and, alas! Love or Song
   No charm to Life's lengthening shadows can lend,
Like a cup of old wine, rich, mellow, and strong,
   And a seat by the fire *tête-à-tête* with a friend.

The Laureate.

BY A——— T———.

Who would not be
The Laureate bold
With his butt of sherry
To keep him merry,
And nothing to do but to pocket his gold

'Tis I would be the Laureate bold!
When the days are hot, and the sun is strong,
I 'd lounge in the gateway all the day long,
With her Majesty's footmen in crimson and gold.
I 'd care not a pin for the waiting-lord;
But I 'd lie on my back on the smooth green sward,
With a straw in my mouth, and an open vest,
And the cool wind blowing upon my breast,
And I 'd vacantly stare at the clear blue sky,
And watch the clouds as listless as I,
            Lazily, lazily!
                6*

And I 'd pick the moss and daisies white,
And chew their stalks with a nibbling bite;
And I 'd let my fancies roam abroad
In search of a hint for a birth-day ode,
   Crazily, crazily!
Oh, that would be the life for me,
With plenty to get and nothing to do,
But to deck a pet poodle with ribbons of blue,
And whistle all day to the Queen's cockatoo,
   Trance-somely, trance-somely,
Then the chambermaids, that clean the rooms,
Would come to the windows and rest on their brooms,
With their saucy caps, and their crisped hair,
And they 'd toss their heads in the fragrant air,
And say to each other—"Just look down there,
At the nice young man, so tidy and small,
Who is paid for writing on nothing at all,
   Handsomely, handsomely!"

They would pelt me with matches and sweet pastilles,
And crumpled up balls of the royal bills,
Giggling and laughing, and screaming with fun,
As they 'd see me start, with a leap and a run,
From the broad of my back to the point of my toes,
When a pellet of paper hit my nose,
   Teazingly, sneezingly.
Then I 'd fling them bunches of garden flowers,
And hyacinths plucked from the Castle bowers;
And I 'd challenge them all to come down to me,
And I 'd kiss them all till they kissed me,
   Laughingly, laughingly.

Oh, would not that be a merry life,
Apart from care, and apart from strife,
With the Laureate's wine, and the Laureate's pay,
And no deductions at quarter-day?
Oh, that would be the post for me!
With plenty to get and nothing to do
But to deck a pet poodle with ribbons of blue,
And whistle a tune to the Queen's cockatoo,
And scribble of verses remarkably few,
And at evening empty a bottle or two,
   Quaffingly, quaffingly!

   'T is I would be
    The Laureate bold,
   With my butt of sherry
   To keep me merry,
And nothing to do but to pocket my gold!

A Midnight Meditation.

BY SIR E——— B——— L———.

FILL me once more the foaming pewter up!
　Another board of oysters, ladye mine!
To-night Lucullus with himself shall sup.
　　These mute inglorious Miltons are divine;
　　And as I here in slippered ease recline,
Quaffing of Perkins' Entire my fill,
I-sigh not for the lymph of Aganippe's rill.

A nobler inspiration fires my brain,
　Caught from Old England's fine time-hallowed drink;
I snatch the pot again and yet again,
　　And as the foaming fluids shrink and shrink,
　　Fill me once more, I say, up to the brink!
This makes strong hearts—strong heads attest its charm—
This nerves the might that sleeps in Britain's brawny
　　arm!

But these remarks are neither here nor there.
　Where was I?　Oh, I see—old Southey 's dead!
They 'll want some bard to fill the vacant chair,
　　And drain the annual butt—and oh, what head
　　More fit with laurel to be garlanded

Than this, which, curled in many a fragrant coil,
Breathes of Castalia's streams, and best Macassar oil ?

I know a grace is seated on my brow,
    Like young Apollo's with his golden beams;
There should Apollo's bays be budding now :
    And in my flashing eyes the radiance beams
    That marks the poet in his waking dreams,
When as his fancies cluster thick and thicker,
He feels the trance divine of poesy and liquor.

They throng around me now, those things of air,
    That from my fancy took their being's stamp :
There Pelham sits and twirls his glossy hair,
    There Clifford leads his pals upon the tramp ;
    Their pale Zanoni, bending o'er his lamp,
Roams through the starry wilderness of thought,
Where all is everything, and everything is nought.

Yes, I am he, who sung how Aram won
    The gentle ear of pensive Madeline !
How love and murder hand in hand may run,
    Cemented by philosophy serene,
    And kisses bless the spot where gore has been !
Who breathed the melting sentiment of crime,
And for the assassin waked a sympathy sublime!

Yes, I am he, who on the novel shed
    Obscure philosophy's enchanting light !
Until the public, wildered as they read,
    Believed they saw that which was not in sight—
    Of course 't was not for me to set them right;

For in my nether heart convinced I am,
Philosophy 's as good as any other bam.

Novels three-volumed I shall write no more—
  Somehow or other now they will not sell ;
And to invent new passions is a bore—
  I find the Magazines pay quite as well.
  Translating 's simple, too, as I can tell,
Who 've hawked at Schiller on his lyric throne,
And given the astonished bard a meaning all my own.

Moore, Campbell, Wordsworth, their best days are
    grassed ;
  Battered and broken are their early lyres.
Rogers, a pleasant memory of the past,
  Warmed his young hands at Smithfield's martyr fires,
  And, worth a plum, nor bays, nor butt desires.
But these are things would suit me to the letter,
For though this Stout is good, old Sherry 's greatly
    better.

A fico for your small poetic ravers,
  Your Hunts, your Tennysons, your Milnes, and these !
Shall they compete with him who wrote "Maltravers,"
  Prologue to "Alice or the Mysteries?"
  No ! Even now, my glance prophetic sees
My own high brow girt with the bays about.
What ho, within there, ho ! another pint of STOUT !

Montgomery.

A POEM.

Like one who, waking from a troublous dream,
Pursues with force his meditative theme;
Calm as the ocean in its halcyon still,
Calm as the sunlight sleeping on the hill:
Calm as at Ephesus great Paul was seen
To rend his robes in agonies serene;
Calm as the love that radiant Luther bore
To all that lived behind him, and before;
Calm as meek Calvin, when, with holy smile,
He sang the mass around Servetus' pile,—
So once again I snatch this harp of mine,
To breathe rich incense from a mystic shrine.
Not now to whisper to the ambient air
The sound of Satan's Universal Prayer;
Not now to sing in sweet domestic strife
That woman reigns the Angel of our life;
But to proclaim the wish, with pious art,
Which thrills through Britain's universal heart,—
That on this brow, with native honors graced,
The Laureate's chaplet should at length be placed!

Fear not, ye maids, who love to hear me speak;
Let no desponding tears bedim your cheek!
No gust of envy, no malicious scorn,
Hath this poor heart of mine with frenzy torn.
There are who move so far above the great,
Their very look disarms the glance of hate;
Their thoughts, more rich than emerald or gold,
Enwrap them like the prophet's mantle's fold.
Fear not for me, nor think that this our age,
Blind though it be, hath yet no Archimage.
I, who have bathed in bright Castalia's tide,
By classic Isis and more classic Clyde;
I, who have handled in my lofty strain,
All things divine, and many things profane;
I, who have trod where seraphs fear to tread;
I, who on mountain — honey dew have fed;
I, who undaunted broke the mystic seal,
And left no page for prophets to reveal;
I, who in shade portentous Dante threw;
I, who have done what Milton dared not do,—
I fear no rival for the vacant throne;
No mortal thunder shall eclipse my own!

Let dark Macaulay chaunt his Roman lays,
Let Monckton Milnes go mounder for the bays,
Let Simmons call on great Napoleon's shade,
Let Lytton Bulwer seek his Aram's aid,
Let Wordsworth ask for help from Peter Bell,
Let Campbell carol Copenhagen's knell,
Let Delta warble through his Delphic groves,
Let Elliot shout for pork and penny loaves,—

I caıe not, I! resolved to stand or fall;
One down, another on, I 'll smash them all!

Back, ye profane! this hand alone hath power
To pluck the laurel from its sacred bower;
This brow alone is privileged to wea.
The ancient wreath o'er hyacinthine hair;
These lips alone may quaff the sparkling wine,
And make its mortal juice once more divine.
Back, ye profane! And thou, fair queen, rejoice:
A nation's praise shall consecrate thy choice.
Thus, then, I kneel where Spencer knelt before,
On the same spot perchance, of Windsor's floor;
And take, while awe-struck millions round me stand,
The hallowed wreath from great Victoria's hand.

The Death of Space.

[WHY has Satan's own Laureate never given to the world his marvellous threnody on "The Death of Space?" Who knows where the bays might have fallen, had he forwarded that mystic manuscript to the Home Office? If unwonted modesty withholds it from the public eye, the public will pardon the boldness that tears from blushing obscurity the following fragments of this unique poem.]

ETERNITY shall raise her funeral pile
   In the vast dungeon of the extinguish'd sky,
And, clothed in dim barbaric splendor, smile,
   And murmur shouts of elegiac joy.

While those that dwell beyond the realms of space,
   And those that people all that dreary void,
When old Time's endless heir hath run his race,
   Shall live for aye, enjoying and enjoy'd.

And 'mid the agony of unsullied bliss,
   Her Demogorgon's doom shall Sin bewail,
The undying serpent at the spheres shall hiss,
   And lash the empyrean with his tail.

And Hell, inflated with supernal wrath,
  Shall open wide her thunder-bolted jaws,
And shout into the dull cold ear of Death,
  That he must pay his debt to Nature's laws.

And when the King of Terrors breathes his last,
  Infinity shall creep into her shell,
Cause and effect shall from their thrones be cast,
  And end their strife with suicidal yell.

While from their ashes, burnt with pomp of Kings
  'Mid incense floating to the evanished skies,
Nonentity, on circumambient wings,
  An everlasting Phœnix shall arise.

Little John and the Red Friar.

A LAY OF SHERWOOD.

FYTTE THE FIRST.

THE deer may leap within the glade;
  The fawns may follow free—
For Robin is dead, and his bones are laid
  Beneath the greenwood tree.

And broken are his merry, merry men,
  That goodlie companie;
There 's some have ta'en the n. rthern road
  With Jem of' Netherbee.

The best and bravest of the band
  With Derby Ned are gone;
But Earlie Gray and Charlie Wood,
  They staid with Little John.

Now Little John was an outlaw proud,
  A prouder ye never saw;
Through Nottingham and Leicester shires
  He thought his word was law,
And he strutted through the greenwood wide
  Like a pestilent jack-daw.

He swore that none, but with leave of him,
  Should set foot on the turf so free ·
And he thought to spread his cutter's rule,
  All over the south countrie.
"There 's never a knave in the land," he said,
  "But shall pay his toll to me!"

And Charlie Wood was a taxman good
  As ever stepped the ground,
He levied mail, like a sturdy thief,
  From all the yeomen round.
"Nay, stand!" quoth he, "thou shalt pay to me,
  Seven pence from every pound!"

Now word has come to Little John,
  As he lay upon the grass,
That a friar red was in merry Sherwood
  Without his leave to pass.

"Come hither, come hither, my little foot-page!
  Ben Hawes, come tell to me,
What manner of man is this burly frere
  Who walks the wood so free!"

"My master good!" the little page said,
  "His name I wot not well,
But he wears on his head a hat so red,
  With a monstrous scallop-shell.

"He says he is Prior of Copmanshurst,
  And Bishop of London town,
And he comes with a rope from our father, the Pope
  To put the outlaws down.

"I saw him ride but yester-tide
    With his jolly chaplains three;
And he swears that he has an open pass
    From Jem of Netherbee!"

Little John has ta'en an arrow so broad,
    And broke it o'er his knee;
"Now I may never strike doe again,
    But this wrong avenged shall be!

"And has he dared, this greasy frere,
    To trespass in my bound,
Nor asked for leave from Little John
    To range with hawk and hound?

"And has he dared to take a pass
    From Jem of Netherbee,
Forgetting that the Sherwood shaws
    Pertain of right to me?

"O were he but a simple man
    And not a slip-shod frere!
I'd hang him up by his own waist-rope
    Above yon tangled brere.

"O did he come alone from Jem
    And not from our father the Pope,
I'd bring him in to Copmanshurst,
    With the noose of a hempen rope!

" But since he has come from our father the Pope,
    And sailed across the sea, ,
And since he has power to bind and loose,
    His life is safe for me ;
But a heavy penance he shall do
·   Beneath the greenwood tree !"

" O tarry yet," quoth Charlie Wood,
    " O tarry, master mine !
It 's ill to shear a yearling hog,
    Or twist the wool of swine !

" It 's ill to make a bonny silk purse
    From the ear of a bristly boar ;
It 's ill to provoke a shaveling's curse,
    When the way lies him before.

" I 've walked the forest for twenty years,
    In weather wet and dry,
And never stopped a good fellawe
    Who had no coin to buy.

" What boots it to search a beggarman's bags
    When no silver groat he has ?
So, master mine, I rede you well,
    E'en let the Friar pass !"

" Now cease thy prate," quoth Little John,
    " Thou japest but in vain ;
An he have not a groat within his pouch
    We may find a silver chain.

" But were he as bare as a new-flayed buck,
    As truly he may be,
He shall not tread the Sherwood shaws
    Without the leave of me !"

" Little John has taken his arrows and bow,
    His sword and buckler strong,
And lifted up his quarter-staff,
    Was full three cloth yards long

And he has left his merry men
    At the trysting-tree behind,
And gone into the gay greenwood,
    This burly frere to find.

O'er holt and hill, thro' brake and brere
    He took his way alone—
Now, Lordlings, list and you shall hear
    This geste of Little John.

FYTTE THE SECOND.

'T is merry, 't is merry in gay greenwood,
    When the little birds are singing,
When the buck is belling in the fern
    And the hare from the thicket springing!

'T is merry to hear the waters clear
    As they splash in the pebbly fall;
And the ouzel whistling to his mate
    As he lights on the stones so small.

But small pleasaunce took little John
  In all he heard and saw;
Till he reached the cave of a hermit old
  Who wonned within the shaw.

" *Ora pro nobis !*" quoth Little John—
  His Latin was somewhat rude—
"Now, holy Father, hast thou seen
  A frere within the wood?

"By his scarlet hose, and his ruddy nose,
  I guess you may know him well;
And he wears on his head a hat so red,
  And monstrous scallop shell."

"I have served Saint Pancras," the hermit said,
  "In this cell for thirty year,
Yet never saw I, in the forest bounds,
  The face of such a frere!

"And if ye find him, master mine,
  E'er take an old man's advice,
And raddle him well, till he roar again,
  Lest ye fail to meet him twice!"

"Trust me for that!" quoth Little John—
  "Trust me for that!" quoth he with a laugh,
"There never was man of woman born,
  That ask'd twice for the taste of my quarter-staff!"

7

Then Little John, he strutted on,
  'Till he came to an open bound,
And he was aware of a Red Friar
  Was sitting upon the ground.

His shoulders they were broad and strong,
  And large was he of limb :
Few yeomen in the north countrie
  Would care to mell with him.

He heard the rustling of the boughs,
  As Little John drew near ;
But never a single word he spoke,
  Of welcome or of cheer.

I like not his looks ! thought Little John,
  Nor his staff of the oaken tree.
Now may our Lady be my help,
  Else beaten I well may be !   .

" What dost thou here, thou strong Friar,
  In Sherwood's merry round,
Without the leave of Little John,
  To range with hawk and hound ?"

" Small thought have I," quoth the Red Friar,
  " Of any leave, I trow.
That Little John is an outlawed thief,
  And so, I ween, art thou !

"Know, 1 am Prior of Copmanshurst,
  And Bishop of London town,
And I bring a rope from our father the Pope,
  To put the outlaws down."

Then out spoke Little John in wrath,
  "I tell thee, burly frere,
The Pope may do as he likes at home,
  But he sends no Bishops here!

"Up, and away, Red Friar!" he said,
  "Up, and away, right speedilie;
An it were not for that cowl of thine,
  Avenged on thy body I would be!"

"Nay, heed not that," said the Red Friar,
  "And let my cowl no hindrance be;
I warrant that I can give as good
  As ever I think to take from thee!"

Little John he raised his quarter-staff,
  And so did the burly priest,
And they fought beneath the greenwood tree,
  A stricken hour at least.

But Little John was weak of fence,
  And his strength began to fail,
Whilst the Friar's blows came thundering down,
  Like the strokes of a threshing flail.

"Now, hold thy hand," thou stalwart Friar,
"Now rest beneath the thorn,
Until I gather breath enow,
For a blast at my bugle horn!"

"I 'll hold my hand," the Friar said,
"Since that is your propine,
But, an you sound your bugle horn,
I 'll even blow on mine!"

Little John he wound a blast so shrill
That it rung o'er rock and linn,
And Charlie Wood and his merry men all
Came lightly bounding in.

The Friar he wound a blast so strong
That it shook both bush and tree,
And to his side came Witless Will
And Jem of Netherbee;
With all the worst of Robin's band,
And many a Rapparee!

Liltle John he wist not what to do,
When he saw the others come;
So he twisted his quarter-staff between
His fingers and his thumb.

"There 's some mistake, good Friar!" he said,
"There 's some mistake 'twixt thee and me;
I know thou art Prior of Copmanshurst,
But not beneath the greenwood tree.

"And if you will take some other name,
    You shall have ample leave to bide;
With pasture also for your Bulls,
    And power to range the forest wide."

"There 's no mistake!" the Friar said,
    "I 'll call myself just what I please.
My doctrine is that chalk is chalk,
    And cheese is nothing else than cheese."

"So be it then!" quoth Little John;
    "But surely you will not object,
If I and all my merry men
    Should treat you with reserved respect?

' We can't call you Prior of Copmanshurst,
    Nor Bishop of London town,
Nor on the grass, as you chance to pass,
    Can we very well kneel down.

"But you 'll send the Pope my compliments,
    And say, as a further hint,
That, within the Sherwood bounds, you saw
Little John, who is the son-in-law
    Of his friend, old Mat-o'-the-Mint!"

So ends this geste of Little John—
    God save our noble Queen!
But, Lordlings, say—is Sherwood now
    What Sherwood once hath been?

The Rhyme of Sir Launcelot Bogle.

A LEGEND OF GLASGOW.

BY MRS. E———— B———— B————.

THERE 's a pleasant place of rest, near a City of the
    West,
  Where its bravest and its best find their grave.
Below the willows weep, and their hoary branches steep
  In the waters still and deep,
                    Not a wave!

And the old Cathedral Wall, so scathed, and gray, and
    tall,
  Like a priest surveying all, stands beyond.
And the ringing of its bell, when the ringers ring it well,
  Makes a kind of tidal swell
                    On the pond!

And there it was I lay, on a beauteous summer's day,
  With the odor of the hay floating by;
And I heard the blackbirds sing, and the bells demurely
    ring,
  Chime by chime, ting by ting,
                    Droppingly.

THE BOOK OF BALLADS.

Then my thoughts went wandering back on a very
  beaten track
To the confine deep and black of the tomb,
And I wondered who he was, that is laid beneath the
  grass,
Where the dandelion has
              Such a bloom.

Then I straightway did espy, with my slantly sloping
  eye,
A carvéd stone hard by, somewhat worn ;
And I read in letters cold—𝕳𝖊𝖗𝖊.𝖑𝖞𝖊𝖘.𝕷𝖆𝖚𝖓𝖈𝖊𝖑𝖔𝖙.𝖞𝖊.𝖇𝖔𝖑𝖉𝖊,
  𝕺𝖋𝖋.𝖞𝖊.𝖗𝖆𝖈𝖊.𝖔𝖋𝖋.𝕭𝖔𝖌𝖎𝖑𝖊.𝖔𝖑𝖉,
              𝕲𝖑𝖆𝖘𝖌𝖔𝖜.𝖇𝖔𝖗𝖓𝖊.

𝕳𝖊.𝖜𝖆𝖑𝖘.𝖆𝖓𝖊.𝖇𝖆𝖎𝖌𝖆𝖚𝖓𝖙.𝖐𝖓𝖞𝖌𝖍𝖙𝖊.𝖒𝖆𝖎𝖘𝖙.𝖙𝖊𝖗𝖗𝖎𝖇𝖑𝖊.𝖎𝖓.𝖋𝖞𝖌𝖍𝖙𝖊. . .
Here the letters failed outright, but I knew
That a stout crusading lord, who had crossed the Jordan's
  ford,
Lay there beneath the sward,
              Wet with dew.

Time and tide they passed away, on that pleasant sum-
  mer's day,
And around me as I lay, all grew old :
Sank the chimneys from the town, and the clouds of
  vapor brown
No longer, like a crown,
              O'er it rolled.

Sank the great Saint Rollux stalk, like a pile of dingy
    chalk
Disappeared the cypress walk, and the flowers.
And a donjon keep arose, that might baffle any foes,
    With its men-at-arms in rows,
                On its towers.

And the flag that flaunted there, showed the grim and
    grizzly bear,
Which the Bogles always wear for their crest.
And I heard the warder call, as he stood upon the wall,
    " Wake ye up! my comrades all,
                From your rest!

" For by the blessed rood, there's a glimpse of armor good
    In the deep Cowcaddens wood, o'er the stream ;
And I hear the stifled hum, of a multitude that come,
    Though they have not beat the drum
                It would seem!

" Go tell it to my Lord, lest he wish to man the ford
    With partizan and sword, just beneath ;
Ho, Gilkison and Nares!   Ho, Provan of Cowlairs !
    We 'll back the bonny bears
                To the death !"

To the tower above the moat, like one who heedeth not,
    Came the bold Sir Launcelot, half undressed ;
On the outer rim he stood, and peered into the wood,
    With his arms across him glued
                On his breast.

And he muttered "Foe accurst! has thou dared to seek
    me first?
George of Gorbals, do thy worst—for I swear,
O'er thy gory corpse to ride, ere thy sister and my
    bride,
    From my undescvered side,
              Thou shalt tear!

"Ho! herald mine, Brownlee! ride forth, I pray and
    see,
Who, what, and whence is he, foe or friend!
Sir Roderick Dalgleish, and my foster-brother Neish
    With his bloodhounds in the leash,
              Shall attend."

Forth went the herald stout, o'er the drawbridge and
    without,
Then a wild and savage shout rose amain,
Six arrows sped their force, and, a pale and bleeding
    corse,
    He sank from off his horse
              On the plain!

Back drew the bold Dalgleish, back started stalwart
    Neish,
With his bloodhounds in the leash, from Brownlee.
"Now shame be to the sword that made thee knight
    and lord,
    Thou caitiff thrice abhorred,
            Shame on thee!
    7*

"Ho, bowmen, bend your bows! Discharge upon the
   foes,
Forthwith no end of those heavy bolts.
Three angels to the brave who finds the foe a grave,
   And a gallows for the slave
                    Who revolts!"

Ten days the combat lasted; but the bold defenders
   fasted,
While the foemen, better pastied, fed their host;
You might hear the savage cheers of the hungry Gorba-
   liers,
   As at night they dressed the steers
                    For the roast.

And Sir Launcelot grew thin, and Provan's double chin
   Showed sundry folds of skin down beneath;
In silence and in grief found Gilkison relief,
   Nor did Neish the spellword, beef,
                    Dare to breathe.

To the ramparts Edith came, that fair and youthful
   dame,
With the rosy evening flame on her face.
She sighed, and looked around on the soldiers on the
   ground,
   Who but little penance found,
                    Saying grace!

And she said unto her lord, as he leaned upon his
    sword,
" One short and little word may I speak ?
I cannot bear to view those eyes so ghastly blue,
    Or mark the sallow hue
                Of thy cheek !

" I know the rage and wrath that my furious brother
    hath
Is less against us both than at me.
Then, dearest, let me go, to find among the foe
    An arrow from the bow,
                Like Brownlee !"

" I would soil my father's name, I would lose my trea-
    sured fame,
Ladye mine, should such a shame on me light:
While I wear a belted brand, together still we
    stand,
    Heart to heart, hand to hand !"
                Said the knight.

" All our chances are not lost, as your brother and his
    host
Shall discover to their cost rather hard !
Ho, Provan ! take this key—hoist up the Malvoisie,
    And heap it, d' ye see,
              In the yard.

"Of usquebaugh and rum, you will find I reckon
    some,
  Besides the beer and mum, extra stout ;
Go straightway to your tasks, and roll me all the
    casks,
  As also range the flasks,
                Just without.

"If I know the Gorbaliers, they are sure to dip their
    ears
  In the very inmost tiers of the drink.
Let them win the outer-court, and hold it for their sport,
  Since their time is rather short,
                I should think !"

With a loud triumphant yell, as the heavy drawbridge
    fell,
  Rushed the Gorbaliers pell-mell, wild as Druids ;
Mad with thirst for human gore, how they threatened
    and they swore,
  Till they stumbled on the floor,
                O'er the fluids!

Down their weapons then they threw, and each savage
    soldier drew
  From his belt an iron screw, in his fist :
George of Gorbals found it vain their excitement to
    restrain,
  And indeed was rather fain
                To assist.

With a beaker in his hand, in the midst he took his
    stand,
  And silence did command all below—
" Ho ! Launcelot the bold, ere thy lips are icy cold,
  In the centre of thy hold,
              Pledge me now !

" Art surly, brother mine ?   In this cup of rosy
    wine,
  I drink to the decline of thy race !
Thy proud career is done, thy sand is nearly run,
  Never more shall setting sun
              Gild thy face !

" The pilgrim in amaze, shall see a goodly blaze,
  Ere the pallid morning rays flicker up.
And perchance he may espy certain corpses swinging
    high !
  What, brother ! art thou dry ?
              Fill my cup !"

Dumb as death stood Launcelot, as though he heard
    him not,
  But his bosom Provan smote, and he swore :
And Sir Roderick Dalgleish, remarked aside to
    Neish,
  " Never sure did thirsty fish
              Swallow more !"

"Thirty casks are nearly done, yet the revel 's scarce
    begun,
    It were knightly sport and fun to strike in !"
"Nay, tarry till they come," quoth Neish, "unto the
    rum—
    They are working at the mum,
                    And the gin !"

Then straight there did appear to each gallant Gorbalier
    Twenty castles dancing near, all around,
The solid earth did shake, and the stones beneath them
    quake,
    And sinuous as a snake
                    Moved the ground.

Why and wherefore they had come, seemed intricate to
    some,
    But all agreed the rum was divine.
And they looked with bitter scorn on their leader highly
    born,
    Who preferred to fill his horn ·
                    Up with wine !

Then said Launcelot the tall, "Bring the chargers from
    their stall ;
    Lead them straight unto the hall, down below :
Draw your weapons from your side, fling the gates
    asunder wide,
    And together we shall ride
                    On the foe !"

Then Provan knew full well, as he leaped into his
    selle,
  That few would 'scape to tell how they fared,
And Gilkison and Nares, both mounted on their mares,
  Looked terrible as bears,
                All prepared.

With his bloodhounds in the leash, stood the iron-sinew-
    ed Neish,
  And the falchion of Dalgleish glittered bright—
" Now, wake the trumpet's blast; and, comrades, follow
    fast;
  Smite them down unto the last!"
                Cried the knight.

In the cumbered yard without, there was shriek, and
    yell, and shout,
  As the warriors wheeled about, all in mail.
On the miserable kerne, fell the death-strokes stiff and
    stern,
  As the deer treads down the fern,
                In the vale!

Saint Mungo be my guide! It was goodly, in that
    tide
  To see the Bogle ride in his haste;
He accompanied each blow, with a cry of " Ha !" or
    " Ho !"
  And always cleft the foe
                To the waist.

" George of Gorbals—craven lord ! thou didst threat me
    with the cord,
Come forth and brave my sword, if you dare !"
But he met with no reply, and never could descry
    The glitter of his eye
                  Anywhere.

Ere the dawn of morning shone, all the Gorbaliers were
    down,
    Like a field of barley mown in the car:
It had done a soldier good, to see how Provan stood,
    With Neish all bathed in blood,
                  Panting near.

" Now ply ye to your tasks—go carry down those
    casks,
    And place the empty flasks on the floor.
George of Gorbals scarce will come, with trumpet and
    with drum,
    To taste our beer and rum
                  Any more !

So they plied them to their tasks, and they carried down
    the casks,
    And replaced the empty flasks on the floor;
But pallid for a week was the cellar master's check,
    For he swore he heard a shriek
                  Through the door.

When the merry Christmas came, and the Yule-log lent
  its flame
  To the face of squire and dame in the hall,
The cellarer went down to tap October brown,
  Which was rather of renown
              'Mongst them all.

He placed the spigot low, and gave the cask a blow.
  But his liquor would not flow through the pin.
"Sure, 't is sweet as honeysuckles!" so he rapped it
  with his knuckles,
  But a sound as if of buckles,
              Clashed within.

"Bring a hatchet, varlets, here!" and they cleft the
  cask of beer;
What a spectacle of fear met their sight!
There George of Gorbals lay, skull and bones all blanched
  and grey,
  In the arms he bore the day
              Of the fight!

I have sung this ancient tale, not, I trust, without avail,
  Though the moral ye may fail to perceive,
Sir Launcelot is dust, and his gallant sword is rust,
  And now, I think, I must
              Take my leave!

Ihe Lay of the Louer's Friend.

[Air—"The days we went a gipsying."]

I would all womankind were dead,
    Or banished o'er the sea;
For they have been a bitter plague
    These last six weeks to me:
It is not that I 'm touched myself,
    For that I do not fear;
No female face hath shown me grace
    For many a bygone year.
        But 't is the most infernal bore,
            Of all the bores I know,
        To have a friend who 's lost his heart
            A short time ago.

Whene'er we steam it to Blackwall,
    Or down to Greenwich run,
To quaff the pleasant cider cup,
    And feed on fish and fun;

Or climb the slopes of Richmond Hill,
　To catch a breath of air :
Then, for my sins, he straight begins
　To rave about his fair.
　　Oh, 't is the most tremendous bore,
　　　Of all the bores I know,
　　To have a friend who 's lost his heart
　　　A short time ago.

In vain you pour into his ear
　Your own confiding grief;
In vain you claim his sympathy,
　In vain you ask relief;
In vain you try to rouse him by
　Joke, repartee, or quiz ;
His sole reply 's a burning sigh,
　And " What a mind it is !"
　　O Lord ! it is the greatest bore,
　　　Of all the bores I know,
　　To have a friend who 's lost his heart
　　　A short time ago.

I've heard her thoroughly described
　A hundred times, I 'm sure ;
And all the while I 've tried to smile,
　And patiently endure ;
He waxes strong upon his pangs,
　And potters o'er his grog ;
And still I say, in a playful way—
　" Why you 're a lucky dog !"

But oh ! it is the heaviest bore,
Of all the bores I know,
To have a friend who's lost his heart
A short time ago.

I really wish he'd do like me
When I was young and strong;
I formed a passion every week,
But never kept it long.
But he has not the sportive mood
That always rescued me,
And so I would all women could
Be banished o'er the sea.
For 't is the most egregious bore,
Of all the bores I know,
To have a friend who's lost his heart
A short time ago.

Francesca Da Rimini.

TO BON GAULTIER.

ARGUMENT.—An impassioned pupil of Leigh Hunt, having met Bon
Gaultier at a Fancy Ball, declares the destructive consequences
thus.]

Didst thou not praise me, Gaultier, at the ball,
Ripe lips, trim boddice, and a waist so small,
With clipsome lightness, dwindling ever less,
Beneath the robe of pea-y greeniness?
Dost thou remember, when with stately prance,
Our heads went crosswise in the country dance;
How soft, warm fingers, tipp'd like buds of balm,
Trembled within the squeezing of thy palm;
And how a cheek grew flush'd and peachy-wise
At the frank lifting of thy cordial eyes?
Ah, me! that night there was one gentle thing,
Who like a dove, with its scarce-feather'd wing,
Flutter'd at the approach of thy quaint swaggering!

There's wont to be, at conscious times like these,
An affectation of a bright-eyed ease,—
A crispy-cheekiness, if so I dare
Describe the swaling of a jaunty air ;
And thus, when swirling from the waltz's wheel,
You craved my hand to grace the next quadrille,
That smiling voice, although it made me start,
Boil'd in the meek o'erlifting of my heart ;
And, picking at my flowers, I said with free
And usual tone, "Oh yes, sir, certainly !"

Like one that swoons, 'twixt sweet amaze and fear,
I heard the music burning in my ear,
And felt I cared not, so thou wert with me,
If Gurth or Wamba were our vis-à-vis.
So, when a tall Knight Templar ringing came,
And took his place against us with his dame,
I neither turned away, nor bashful shrunk
From the stern survey of the soldier-monk,
Though rather more than full three-quarters drunk ;
But threading through the figure, first in rule,
I paused to see thee plunge into La Poule.

Ah, what a sight was that ?   Not prurient Mars,
Pointing his toe through ten celestial bars—
Not young Apollo, beamily array'd
In tripsome guise for Juno's masquerade—
Not smartest Hermes, with his pinion girth,
Jerking with freaks and snatches down to earth,
Look'd half so bold, so beautiful and strong,
As thou when pranking thro' the glittering throng!

How the calm'd ladies looked with eyes of love
On thy trim velvet doublet laced above ;
The hem of gold, that, like a wavy river,
Flowed down into thy back with glancing shiver!
So bare was thy fine throat, and curls of black
So lightsomely dropp'd on thy lordly back,
So crisply swaled the feather in thy bonnet,
So glanced thy thigh, and spanning palm upon it,
That my weak soul took instant flight to thee,
Lost in the fondest gush of that sweet witchery!

But when the dance was o'er, and arm in arm,
(The full heart beating 'gainst the elbow warm,)
We pass'd into the great refreshment-hall,
Where the heap'd cheese-cakes and the comfits small
Lay, like a hive of sunbeams, brought to burn
Around the margin of the negus urn ;
When my poor quivering hand you finger'd twice,
And, with enquiring accents, whisper'd "Ice,
Water, or cream ?"   I could no more dissemble,
But dropp'd upon the couch all in a tremble.
A swimming faintness misted o'er my brain,
The corks seem'd starting from the brisk champagne,
The custards fell untouch'd upon the floor,
Thine eyes met mine.   That night we danced no more!

The Cadi's Daughter.

A LEGEND OF THE BOSPHORUS.

How beauteous is the star of night
  Within the eastern skies,
Like the twinkling glance of the Toorkman's lance,
  Or the antelope's azure eyes!
A lamp of love in the heaven above,
  That star is fondly streaming;
And the gay kiosk and the shadowy mosque
  In the Golden Horn are gleaming.
Young Leila sits in her jasmine bower,
  And she hears the bulbul sing,
As it thrills its throat to the first full note,
  That anthems the flowery spring.
She gazes still, as a maiden will,
  On that beauteous eastern star :
You might see the throb of her bosom's sob
  Beneath the white cymar!

She thinks of him who is far away,—
  Her own brave Galiongee,—
Where the billows foam and the breezes roam,
  On the wild Carpathian sea.

She thinks of the oath that bound them both
  Beside the stormy water;
And the words of love, that in Athens' grove
  He spake to the Cadi's daughter.

"My Selim!" thus the maiden said,
  "Though severed thus we be,
By the raging deep and the mountains' steep,
  My soul still yearns to thee.
Thy form so dear is mirror'd here
  In my heart's pellucid well,
As the rose looks up to Phingari's orb,
  Or the moth to 'the gay gazelle.

"I think of the time, when the Kaftan's crime
  Our love's young joys o'ertook,
And thy name still floats in the plaintive notes
  Of my silver-toned chibouque.
Thy hand is red with the blood it has shed,
  Thy soul it is heavy laden;
Yet come, my Giaour, to thy Leila's bower;
  Oh, come to thy Turkish maiden!"

A light step trode on the dewy sod,
  And a voice was in her ear,
And an arm embraced young Leila's waist—
  "Belovéd! I am here!"
Like the phantom form that rules the storm,
  Appeared the pirate lover,
And his fiery eye was like Zatanai,
  As he fondly bent above her.

"Speak, Leila, speak! for my light caïque
    Rides proudly in yonder bay;
I have come from my rest to her I love best,
    To carry thee, love, away.
The breast of thy lover shall shield thee, and cover
    My own jemscheed from harm;
Think'st thou I fear the dark vizier,
    Or the mufti's vengeful arm?

"Then droop not, love, nor turn away
    From this rude hand of mine!"
And Leila looked in her lover's eyes,
    And murmured—"I am thine!"
But a gloomy man with a yataghan
    Stole through the acacia blossoms,
And the thrust he made with his gleaming blade
    Had pierced through both their bosoms.

"There! there! thou curséd caitiff Giaour!
    There, there, thou false one, lie!"
Remorseless Hassan stands above,
    And he smiles to see them die.
They sleep beneath the fresh green turf,
    The lover and the lady—
And the maidens wail to hear the tale
    Of the daughter of the Cadi!

Eastern Serenade.

THE minarets wave on the plain of Stamboul,
And the breeze of the evening blows freshly and cool;
The voice of the musnud is heard from the west,
And kaftan and kalpac have gone to their rest,
The notes of the kislar re-echo no more,
And the waves of Al Sirat fall light on the shore.

Where art thou, my beauty; where art thou, my bride?
Oh, come and repose by the dragoman's side!
I wait for thee still by the flowery tophaik—
I have broken my Eblis for Zuleima's sake.
But the heart that adores thee is faithful and true,
Though it beats 'neath the folds of a Greek Allah-hu!

Oh, wake thee, my dearest! the muftis are still.
And the tschocadars sleep on the Franguestan hill;
No sullen aleikoum—no derveesh is here,
And the mosques are all watching by lonely Kashmere!
Oh, come in the gush of thy beauty so full,
I have waited for thee, my adored attar-gul!

I see thee—I hear thee—thy antelope foot
Treads lightly and soft on the velvet cheroot;
The jewelled amaun of thy zemzem is bare,
And the folds of thy palampore wave in the air.
Come, rest on the bosom that loves thee so well,
My dove! my phingari! my gentle gazelle!

Nay, tremble not, dearest!   I feel thy heart throb,
'Neath the sheltering shroud of thy snowy kiebaub;
Lo, there shines Muezzin, the beautiful star!
Thy lover is with thee, and danger afar:
Say, is it the glance of the haughty vizier,
Or the bark of the distant effendi, you fear?

Oh, swift fly the hours in the garden of bliss!
And sweeter than balm of Gehenna, thy kiss!
Wherever I wander—wherever I roam,
My spirit flies back to its beautiful home:
It dwells by the lake of the limpid Stamboul,
With thee, my adored one! my own attar-gul!

The Death of Duval.

BY W———H———A———TH, ESQ.

"Methinks I see him already in the cart, sweeter and more lovely than the nosegay in his hand! I hear the crowd extolling his resolution and intrepidity! What volleys of sighs are sent from the windows of Holborn, that so comely a youth should be brought to disgrace! I see him at the tree! the whole circle are in tears! even butchers weep!"—BEGGAR'S OPERA.

A LIVING sea of eager human faces,
   A thousand bosoms, throbbing all as one,
Walls, windows, balconies, all sorts of places,
   Holding their crowds of gazers to the sun :
     Through the hushed groups low buzzing murmurs run ;
And on the air, with slow reluctant swell,
Comes the dull funeral boom of old Sepulchre's bell.

Oh, joy in London now ! in festal measure
   Be spent the evening of this festive day !
For thee is opening now a high-strung pleasure
   Now, even now, in yonder press-yard they
     Strike from his limbs the fetters loose away !
A little while, and he, the brave Duval,
Will issue forth, serene, to glad and greet you all.

"Why comes he not? say, wherefore doth he tarry?"
Starts the enquiry loud from every tongue.
"Surely," they cry, "that tedious Ordinary
His tedious psalms must long ere this have sung,—
Tedious to him that's waiting to be hung!"
But hark! old Newgate's doors fly wide apart.
"He comes, he comes!" A thrill shoots through each
gazer's heart.

Join'd in the stunning cry ten thousand voices,
All Smithfield answered to the loud acclaim.
"He comes, he comes!" and every breast rejoices,
As down Snow Hill the shout tumultuous came,
Bearing to Holborn's crowd the welcome fame.
"He comes, he comes!" and each holds back his
breath,—
Some ribs are broke and some few scores are crush'd to
death.

With step majestic to the cart advances
The dauntless Claude, and springs into his seat.
He feels that on him now are fix'd the glances
Of many a Britain bold and maiden sweet,
Whose hearts responsive to his glories beat.
In him the honor of "The Road" is centred,
And all the hero's fire into his bosom enter'd.

His was the transport—his the exultation
Of Rome's great generals, when from afar,
Up to the Capitol, in the ovation,

They bore with them in the triumphal car,
  Rich gold and gems, the spoils of foreign war.
Io Triumphe! They forgot their clay.
E'en so Duval who rode in glory on his way.

His laced cravat, his kids of purest yellow,
  The many-tinted nosegay in his hand,
His large black eyes, so fiery, yet so mellow,
  Like the old vintages of Spanish land,
  Locks clustering o'er a brow of high command,
Subdue all hearts ; and, as up Holborn's steep
Toils the slow car of death, e'en cruel butchers weep.

He saw it, but he heeded not. His story,
  He knew, was graven on the page of Time.
Tyburn to him was as a field of glory,
  Where he must stoop to death his head sublime,
  Hymn'd in full many an elegiac rhyme.
He left his deeds behind him, and his name—
For he, like Cæsar, had lived long enough for fame.

He quail'd not, save when, as he raised the chalice,—
  St. Giles's bowl,—filled with the mildest ale,
To pledge the crowd, on her—his beauteous Alice—
  His eye alighted, and his cheek grew pale.
  She, whose sweet breath was like the spicy gale,
She, whom he fondly deem'd his own dear girl,
Stood with a tall dragoon, drinking long draughts of
    purl.

He bit his lip—it quiver'd but a moment—
  Then pass'd his hand across his flashing brows :
He could have spared so forcible a comment
  Upon the constancy of woman's vows.
  One short, sharp pang his hero-soul allows ;
But in the bowl he drowned the stinging pain,
And on his pilgrim-course went calmly forth again.

A princely group of England's noble daughters
  Stood in a balcony suffused with grief,
Diffusing fragrance round them, of strong waters,
  And waving many a snowy handkerchief.
  Then glow'd the prince of highwayman and thief!
His soul was touched with a seraphic gleam :—
That woman could be false was but a mocking dream.

And now, his bright career of triumph ended,
  His chariot stood beneath the triple tree.
The law's grim finisher to its boughs ascended,
  And fix'd the hempen bandages, while he
  Bow'd to the throng, then bade the car go free.
The car roll'd on, and left him dangling there
Like famed Mahommed's tomb, uphung midway in air

As droops the cup of the surcharged lily
  Beneath the buffets of the surly storm,
Or the soft petals of the daffodilly,
  When Sirius is uncomfortably warm,
  So drooped his head upon his manly form,
While floated in the breeze his tresses brown.
He hung the stated time, and then they cut him down.

With soft and tender care the trainbands bore him,
    Just as they found him, nightcap, rope, and all,
And placed this neat though plain inscription o'er him,
    Among the otomies in Surgeon's Hall :
    "THESE ARE THE BONES OF THE RENOWN'D DUVAL!"
There still they tell us, from their glassy case,
He was the last, the best of all that noble race !

The Dirge of the Drinker.

BY W—— E—— A——, ESQ.

BROTHERS, spare awhile your liquor, lay your final tum-
 bler down;
He has dropp'd—that star of honor—on the field of his
 renown!
Raise the wail, but raise it softly, lowly bending on your
 knees,
If you find it more convenient, you may hiccup if you
 please.
Sons of Pantagruel, gently let your hip-hurraing sink,
Be your manly accents clouded, half with sorrow, half
 with drink!
Lightly to the sofa pillow lift his head from off the floor;
See, how calm he sleeps, unconscious as the deadest nail
 in door!
Widely o'er the earth I've wander'd; where the drink
 most freely flow'd,
I have ever reel'd the foremost, foremost to the beaker
 strode.

Deep in shady Cider Cellars I have dream'd o'er heavy
wet,

By the fountains of Damascus I have quaff'd the ricl
Sherbet,

Regal Montepulciano drained beneath its native rock,

On Johannis' sunny mountain frequent hiccup'd o'er my
hock;

I have bathed in butts of Xeres deeper than did e'er
Monsoon,

Sangaree'd with bearded Tartars in the Mountains of the
Moon;

In beer-swilling Copenhagen I have drunk your Danes-
man blind,

I have kept my feet in Jena, when each bursch to earth
declined;

Glass for glass, in fierce Jamaica, I have shared the
planter's rum,

Drank with Highland dhuinie-wassels, till each gibbering
Gael grew dumb;

But a stouter, bolder drinker—one that loved his liquor
more—

Never yet did I encounter than our friend upon the
floor!

Yet the best of us are mortal, we to weakness all are heir,

He has fallen, who rarely stagger'd—let the rest of us
beware!

We shall leave him, as we found him,—lying where his
manhood fell,

'Mong the trophies of the revel, for he took his tipple
well.

Better 't were we loosed his neckcloth, laid his throat
and bosom bare,
Pulled his Hobies off, and turn'd his toes to taste the
breezy air.
Throw the sofa cover o'er him, dim the flaring of the
gas,
Calmly, calmly let him slumber, and, as by the bar we
pass,
We shall bid that thoughtful waiter place beside him,
near and handy,
Large supplies of soda water, tumbler's bottomed well
with brandy,
So when waking, he shall drain them, with that deathless
thirst of his,
Clinging to the hand that smote him, like a good 'un as
he is!

Dame Fredegonde.

WHEN folks with headstrong passion blind,
To play the fool make up their mind,
They 're sure to come with phrases nice,
And modest air, for your advice.
But, as a truth unfailing make it,
They ask, but never mean to take it.
'T is not advice they want, in fact,
But confirmation in their act.
Now mark what did, in such a case,
A worthy priest who knew the race.

A dame more buxsome, blithe and free,
Than Fredegonde you scarce would see.
So smart her dress, so trim her shape,
Ne'er hostess offer'd juice of grape,
Could for her trade wish better sign ;
Her looks gave flavor to her wine,
And each guest feels it, as he sips,
Smack of the ruby of her lips.
A smile for all, a welcome glad,—
A jovial coaxing way she had ;

And,—what was more her fate than blame,—
A nine months' widow was our dame.
But toil was hard, for trade was good,
And gallants sometimes will be rude.
" And what can a lone woman do ?
The nights are long, and eerie too.
Now, Guillot there 's a likely man.
None better draws or taps a can ;
He 's just the man, I think, to suit,
If I could bring my courage to 't."
With thoughts like these her mind is cross'd :
The dame, they say, who doubts is lost.
" But then the risk?   I'll beg a slice
Of Father Raulin's good advice."

    Prankt in her best, with looks demure,
She seeks the priest; and, to be sure,
Asks if he thinks she ought to wed :
" With such a business on my head,
I 'm worried off my legs with care,
And need some help to keep things square.
I 've thought of Guillot, truth to tell !
He 's steady, knows his business well.
What do you think?"   When thus he met her:
" Oh, take him, dear, you can't do better!"
" But then the danger, my good pastor,
If of the man I make the master.
There is no trusting to these men."
" Well, well, my dear, don't have him then!"
" But help I must have, there 's the curse.
I may go farther and fare worse."

" Why, take him then !"   " But if he should
Turn out a thankless ne'er-do-good,—
In drink and riot waste my all,
And rout me out of house and˙hall ?"
" Don't have him, then !   But I 've a plan
To clear your doubts, if any can.
The bells a peal are ringing,—hark !
Go straight, and what they tell you mark.
If they say ' Yes !' wed, and be blest—
If ' No,' why—do as you think best."

The bells rung out a triple bob :
Oh, how our widow's heart did throb,
As thus she heard their burden go,
" Marry, mar-marry, mar-Guillot !"
Bells were not then left to hang idle :
A week,—and the rang for her bridal.
But, woe the while, they might as well
Have rung the poor dame's parting knell.
The rosy dimples left her cheek,
She lost her beauties plump and sleek ;
For Guillot oftener kicked than kiss'd
And back'd his orders with his fist,
Proving by deeds as well as words,
That servants make the worst of lords.

She seeks the priest, her ire to wreak,
And speaks as angry women speak,
With tiger looks, and bosom swelling,
Cursing the hour she took his telling.

To all, his calm reply was this,—
"I fear you 've read the bells amiss.
If they have led you wrong in aught,
Your wish, not they, inspired the thought.
Just go, and mark well what they say."
Off trudged the dame upon her way,
And sure enough their chime went so,—
"Don't have that knave, that knave Guillot!"

"Too true," she cried, "there 's not a doubt:
What could my ears have been about!"
She had forgot, that, as fools think,
The bell is ever sure to clink.

The Death of Ishmael.

[This and the six following poems are examples of that new achievement of modern song—which, blending the *utile* with the *dulce*, symbolizes at once the practical and spiritual characteristics of the age,—and is called familiarly "the puff poetical."]

DIED the Jew? "The Hebrew died.
On the pavement cold he lay,
Around him closed the living tide;
The butcher's cad set down his tray:
The pot-boy from the Dragon Green
No longer for his pewter calls;
The Nereid rushes in between,
Nor more her ' Fine live mackerel!' bawls."

Died the Jew? "The Hebrew died.
They raised him gently from the stone,
They flung his coat and neckcloth wide—
But linen had that Hebrew none.
They raised the pile of hats that pressed
His noble head, his locks of snow;
But, ah, that head, upon his breast,
Sank down with an expiring ' Clo !' "

Died the Jew?   "The Hebrew died,
　　Struck with overwhelming qualms,
From the flavor spreading wide
　　Of some fine Virginia Hams.
Would you know the fatal spot,
　　Fatal to that child of sin ?
These fine-flavored hams are bought
　　At 50, Bishopsgate Within !"

Parr's Life Pills.

'T was in the town of Lubeck.
    A hundred years ago.
An old man walk'd into the church
    With beard as white as snow;
Yet were his cheeks not wrinkled,
    Nor dim his eagle eye:
There's many a knight that steps the street,
Might wonder, should he chance to meet
    That man erect and high!

When silenced was the organ,
    And hush'd the vespers loud,
The Sacristan approached the sire,
    And drew him from the crowd—
" There's something in thy visage,
    On which I dare not look,   ￮
And when I rang the passing bell,
A tremor that I may not tell,
    My very vitals shook.

" Who art thou, awful stranger ?
    Our ancient annals say,
That twice two hundred years ago
    Another passed this way,
Like thee in face and feature ;
    And, if the tale be true,
'T is writ, that in this very year
Again the stranger shall appear.
    Art thou the wandering Jew ?"

" The wandering Jew, thou dotard !"
    The wondrous phantom cried—
'T is several centuries ago
    Since that poor stripling died.
He would not use my nostrums—
    See, shaveling, here they are !
These put to flight all human ills,
These conquer death—unfailing pills,
    And I 'm the inventor, PARR !"

Tarquin and the Augur.

GINGERLY is good King Tarquin shaving,
   Gently glides the razor o'er his chin,
Near him stands a grim Haruspex raving,
   And with nasal whine he pitches in
      Church Extension hints,
      Till the monarch squints,
Snicks his chin, and swears—a deadly sin!

" Jove confound thee, thou bare-legg'd impostor!
   From my dressing-table get thee gone !
Dost thou think my flesh is double Glo'ster ?
   There again!   That cut was to the bone!
      Get ye from my sight;
      I 'll believe you 're right
When my razor cuts the sharping hone !"

Thus spoke Tarquin with a deal of dryness;
   But the Augur, eager for his fees,
Answered—" Try it, your Imperial Highness,
   Press a little harder, if you please.

There ! the deed is done !"
Through the solid stone
Went the steel as glibly as through cheese.

So the Augur touch'd the tin of Tarquin,
    Who suspected some celestial aid :
But he wronged the blameless Gods ; for hearken !
    Ere the monarch's bet was rashly laid,
        With his seaching eye
        Did the priest espy
RODGERS' name engraved upon the blade.

La Mort D'Arthur.

NOT BY ALFRED TENNYSON.

SLOWLY, as one who bears a mortal hurt,
Through which the fountain of his life runs dry,
Crept good King Arthur down unto the lake.
A roughening wind was bringing in the waves
With cold, dull plash and plunging to the shore,
And a great bank of clouds came sailing up
Athwart the aspect of the gibbous moon,
Leaving no glimpse save starlight, as he sank,
With a short stagger, senseless on the stones.

No man yet knows how long he lay in swound;
But long enough it was to let the rust
Lick half the surface of his polished shield;
For it was made by far inferior hands
Than forged his helm, his breastplate, and his greaves,
Whereon no canker lighted, for they bore
The magic stamp of MECHI's SILVER STEEL.

Jupiter and the Indian Ale.

"TAKE away this clammy nectar !"
  Said the king of gods and men ;
"Never at Olympus' table
  Let that trash be served again.
Ho, Lyæus, thou, the beery !
  Quick—invent some other drink ;
Or, in a brace of shakes, thou standest
  On Cocytus' sulphury brink !"

Terror shook the limbs of Bacchus,
  Paly grew his pimpled nose,
And already in his rearward
  Felt he Jove's tremendous toes ;
When a bright idea struck him—
  "Dash my thyrsus ! I 'll be bail—
For you never were in India—
  That you know not HODGSON'S ALE !"

"Bring it!" quoth the Cloud-compeller;
   And the wine-god brought the beer—
"Port and Claret are like water
   To the noble stuff that's here!"
And Saturnius drank and nodded,
   Winking with his lightning eyes;
And amidst the constellations
   Did the star of HODGSON rise!

The Lay of the Doudney Brothers.

COATS at five-and-forty shillings! trousers ten-and-six a
  pair!
Summer waistcoats, three a sovereign, light and comfort-
  able wear!
Taglionis, black or colored, Chesterfield and velveteen!
The old English shooting-jacket,—doeskins, such as ne'er
  were seen!
Army cloaks and riding-habits, Alberts at a trifling cost!
Do you want an annual contract? Write to DOUDNEY's
  by the post.
DOUDNEY BROTHERS! DOUDNEY BROTHERS! Not the
  men that drive the van,
Plaster'd o'er with advertisements, heralding some paltry
  plan,
How, by base mechanic measure, and by pinching of
  their backs,
Slim attorneys' clerks may manage to retrieve their
  Income-tax:
But the old established business—where the best of
  clothes are given
At the very lowest prices—Fleet-street, Number Ninety-
  seven.

Would'st thou know the works of Doudney? Hie thee
to the thronged Arcade,
To the Park upon a Sunday, to the terrible Parade.
There, amid the bayonets bristling, and the flashing of
the steel,
When the household troops in squadrons round the bold
field-marshals wheel,
Should'st thou see an aged warrior in a plain blue morn-
ing frock,
Peering at the proud battalion o'er the margin of his
stock,—
Should thy throbbing heart then tell thee, that the vete-
ran, worn an gray,
Curbed the course of Bonaparte, rolled the thunders of
Assaye—
Let it tell thee, stranger, likewise, that the goodly garb
he wears
Started into shape and being from the DOUDNEY BRO-
THERS' shears!
Seek thou next the rooms of Willis—mark, where
D'Orsay's Count is bending,
See the trousers' undulation from his graceful hip
descending;
Hath the earth another trouser so compact and love-
compelling?
Thou canst find it, stranger, only, if thou seek'st the
DOUDNEYS' dwelling.
Hark, from Windsor's royal palace, what sweet voice
enchants the ear?
"Goodness, what a lovely waistcoat? Oh, who made
it, Albert, dear?

'T is the very prettiest pattern !   You must get a dozen
　　others !"
And the Prince, in rapture, answers—" 'T is the work
　　of Doudney Brothers !"

Paris and Helen.

As the youthful Paris presses
  Helen to his ivory breast,
Sporting with her golden tresses,
  Close and ever closer pressed,

He said : "So let me quaff the nectar,
  Which thy lips of ruby yield ;
Glory I can leave to Hector,
  Gathered in the tented field.

"Let me ever gaze upon thee,
  Look into thine eyes so deep ;
With a daring hand I won thee,
  With a faithful heart I'll keep.

"Oh, my Helen, thou bright wonder,
  Who was ever like to thee ?
Jove would lay aside his thunder,
  So he might be blest like me.

" How mine eyes so fondly linger
    On thy soft and pearly skin ;
Scan each round and rosy finger,
    Drinking draughts of beauty in !

" Tell me, whence thy beauty, fairest !
    Whence thy cheek's enchanting bloom ?
Whence the rosy hue thou wearest,
    Breathing round thee rich perfume ?"

Thus he spoke, with heart that panted,
    Clasped her fondly to his side,
Gazed on her with look enchanted,
    While his Helen thus replied :

" Be no discord, love, between us,   ·
    If I not the secret tell !
'T was a gift I had of Venus,—
    Venus, who hath loved me well.

" And she told me as she gave it,
    ' Let not e'er the charm be known,
O'er thy person freely lave it,
    Only when thou art alone.'

" 'T is enclosed in yonder casket—
    Here behold its golden key ;
But its name—love, do not ask it,
 · Tell 't, I may not, even to thee !"

Long with vow and kiss he plied her,
  Still the secret did she keep,
Till at length he sank beside her,
  Seemed as he had dropped to sleep.

Soon was Helen laid in slumber,
  When her Paris, rising slow,
Did his fair neck disencumber
  From her rounded arms of snow;

Then her heedless fingers oping,
  Takes the key and steals away,
To the eben table groping,
  Where the wondrous casket lay;

Eagerly the lid uncloses,
  Sees within it, laid aslope,
PEAR's LIQUID BLOOM OF ROSES,
  Cakes of his TRANSPARENT SOAP!

Song of the Ennuye.

I 'M weary, and sick, and disgusted
  With Britain's mechanical din ;
Where I 'm much too well known to be trusted,
  And plaguily pestered for tin ;
Where love has two eyes for your banker,
  And one chilly glance for yourself;
Where souls can afford to be franker,
  But when they 're well garnished with pelf.

I 'm sick of the whole race of poets,
  Emasculate, missy, and fine ;
They brew their small beer, and don't know its
  Distinction from full-bodied wine.
I 'm sick of the prosers, that house up
  At drowsy St. Stephen's,—ain't you ?
I want some strong spirits to rouse up
  A good revolution or two !

I 'm sick of a land, where each morrow
  Repeats the dull tale of to-day,
Where you can't even find a new sorrow,
  To chase your stale pleasures away.

I 'm sick of blue-stockings horrific,
  Steam, railroads, gas, scrip, and consols;
So I 'll off where the golden Pacific
  Round islands of paradise rolls.

There the passions shall revel unfettered,
  And the heart never speak but in truth,
And the intellect wholly unlettered,
  Be bright with the freedom of youth;
There the earth can rejoice in her blossoms,
  Unsullied by vapor or soot,
And there chimpanzees and opossums
  Shall playfully pelt me with fruit.

There I 'll sit with my dark Orianas,
  In groves by the murmuring sea,
And they 'll give, as I suck the bananas,
  Their kisses, nor ask them from me.
They 'll never torment me for sonnets,
  Nor bore me to death with their owl ;
They 'll ask not for shawls nor for bonnets,
  For milliners there are unknown.

There my couch shall be earth's freshest flowers,
  My curtains the night and the stars,
And my spirit shall gather new powers,
  Uncramped by conventional bars.
Love for love, truth for truth ever giving,
  My days shall be manfully sped;
I shall know that I 'm loved while I 'm living,
  And be wept by fond eyes when I 'm dead!

9*

Caroline.

LIGHTSOME, brightsome, cousin mine.
  Easy, breezy Caroline!
With thy locks all raven-shaded,
From thy merry brow up-braided,
And thine eyes of laughter full,
  Brightsome cousin mine!
Thou in chains of love hast bound me—
Wherefore dost thou flit around me,
  Laughter-loving Caroline?

When I fain would go to sleep
  In my easy chair,
Wherefore on my slumbers creep—
Wherefore start me from repose,
Tickling of my hookèd nose,
  Pulling of my hair?
Wherefore, then, if thou dost love me,
So to words of anger move me,
  Corking of this face of mine,
  Tricksy cousin Caroline!

When a sudden sound I hear,
Much my nervous system suffers,
  Shaking through and through,—
Cousin Caroline, I fear,
  'T was no other, now, but you
Put gunpowder in the snuffers,
  Springing such a mine!
Yes, it was your tricksy self,
Wicked-trickèd, little elf,
  Naughty cousin Caroline!

Pins she sticks into my shoulder,
  Places needles in my chair,
And, when I begin to scold her,
  Tosses back her combèd hair,
  With so saucy-vexed an air,
That the pitying beholder
Cannot brook that I should scold her:
Then again she comes, and bolder,
  Blacks anew this face of mine,
  Artful cousin Caroline!

Would she only say she 'd love me,
  Winsome tinsome Caroline,
Unto such excess 't would move me,
  Teasing, pleasing, cousin mine!
That she might the live-long day
Undermine the snuffer tray,
Tickle still my hookèd nose,
Startle me from calm repose

With her pretty persecution;
Throw the tongs against my shins,
Run me through and through with pins,
   Like a piercéd cushion;
Would she only say she 'd love me,
Darning needles should not move me;
But reclining back, I 'd say,
"Dearest! there 's the snuffer tray;
Pinch, O pinch those legs of mine!
   Cork me, cousin Caroline!"

To a Forget-Me-Not.

FOUND IN MY EMPORIUM CF LOVE TOKENS.

SWEET flower, that with thy soft blue eye
　　Did'st once look up in shady spot,
To whisper to the passer-by
　　Those tender words—Forget-me-not!

Though withered now, thou art to me
　　The minister of gentle thought,—
And I could weep to gaze on thee,
　　Love's faded pledge—Forget-me-not!

Thou speak'st of hours when I was young,
　　And happiness arose unsought,
When she, the whispering woods among,
　　Gave me thy bloom—Forget-me-not!

What rapturous hour with that dear maid
　　From memory's page no time shall blot,
When, yielding to my kiss, she said,
　　"Oh, Theodore—Forget-me-not!"

Alas, for love ! alas, for truth !
   Alas for man's uncertain lot !
Alas for all the hopes of youth
   That fade like thee—Forget-me-not !

Alas ! for that one image fair,
   With all my brightest dreams inwrought !
That walks beside me everywhere,
   Still whispering—Forget-me-not !

Oh, memory ! thou art but a sigh
   For friendships dead and loves forgot ;
And many a cold and altered eye,
   That once did say—Forget-me-not !

And I must bow me to thy laws,
   For—odd although it may be thought—
I can't tell who the deuce it was
   That gave me this Forget-me-not !

The Mishap.

"Why art thou weeping, sister?
  Why is thy cheek so pale?
Look up, dear Jane, and tell me
  What is it thou dost ail?

"I know thy will is froward,
  Thy feelings warm and keen,
And that *that* Augustus Howard
  For weeks has not been seen.

"I know how much you loved him;
  But I know thou dost not weep
For him;—for though his passion be,
  His purse is noways deep.

"Then tell me why those teardrops;
  What means this woful mood?
Say, has the tax-collector
  Been calling, and been rude?

" Or has that hateful grocer,
  The slave ! been here to-day ?
Of course he had, by morrow's noon,
  A heavy bill to pay !

" Come, on thy brother's bosom
  Unburden all thy woes ;
Look up, look up, sweet sister ;
  There, dearest, blow your nose."

" Oh, John, 't is not the grocer,
  For his account ; although
How ever he is to be paid,
  I really do not know.

" 'T is not the tax-collector ;
  Though by his fell command,   ·
They 've seized our old paternal clock,
  And new umbrella-stand :

" Nor *that* Augustus Howard,
  Whom I despise almost,—
But the soot's come down the chimney, John,
  And fairly spoiled the roast !"

Comfort in Affliction.

" Wherefore starts my bosom's lord?
Why this anguish in thine eye?
Oh, it seems as thy heart's chord
  Had broken with that sigh.

" Rest thee, my dear lord, I pray,
Rest thee on my bosom now!
And let me wipe the dews away,
  Are gathering on thy brow.

" There, again! that fevered start!
What, love! husband! is thy pain?
There is a sorrow on thy heart,
  A weight upon thy brain!

" Nay, nay, that sickly smile can ne'er
Deceive affection's searching eye;
'T is a wife's duty, love, to share
  Her husband's agony.

"Since the dawn began to peep,
    Have I lain with stifled breath;
Heard thee moaning in thy sleep,
    As thou wert at grips with death.

"Oh, what joy it was to see
    My gentle lord once more awake!
Tell me, what is amiss with thee?
    Speak, or my heart will break!"

"Mary, thou angel of my life,
    Thou ever good and kind;
'T is not, believe me, my dear wife,
    The anguish of the mind!

"It is not in my bosom dear,
    No, nor my brain, in sooth;
But Mary, oh, I feel it here,
    Here in my wisdom tooth!

"Then give,—oh, first, best antidote,—
    Sweet partner of my bed!
Give me thy flannel petticoat
    To wrap around my head!"

The Invocation.

"BROTHER, thou art very weary,
  And thine eye is sunk and dim,
And thy neckcloth's tie is crumpled,
  And thy collar out of trim ;
There is dust upon thy visage,—
  Think not Charles I would hurt ye,
When I say, that altogether,
  You appear extremely dirty.

"Frown not, brother, now, but hie thee
  To thy chamber's distant room ;
Drown the odors of the ledger
  With the lavender's perfume.
Brush the mud from off thy trowsers,
  O'er the china basin kneel,
Lave thy brows in water softened
  With the soap of Old Castile.

"Smooth the locks that o'er thy forehead
  Now in loose disorder stray ;
Pare thy nails, and from thy whiskers
  Cut those ragged points away.

Let no more thy calculations
 Thy bewildered brain beset;
Life has other hopes than Cocker's,
 Other joys than tare and tret.

" Haste thee, for I ordered dinner,
 Waiting to the very last,
Twenty minutes after seven,
 And 't is now the quarter past.
'T is a dinner which Lucullus
 Would have wept with joy to see,
One, might wake the soul of Curtis
 From Death's drowsy atrophy.

" There is soup of real turtle,
 Turbot, and the dainty sole;
And the mottled roe of lobsters
 Blushes through the butter bowl.
There the lordly haunch of mutton,
 Tender as the mountain grass,
·Waits to mix its ruddy juices
 With the girdling caper-sauce.

" There a stag, whose branching forehead
 Spoke him monarch of the herds,
He whose flight was o'er the heather,
 Swift as through the air the bird's,
Yields for thee a dish of cutlets;
 And the haunch that wont to dash
O'er the roaring mountain torrent,
 Smokes in most delicious hash.

"There, besides, arc amber jellies
 Floating like a golden dream;
Ginger from the far Bermudas
 Dishes of Italian cream;
And a princely apple-dumpling,
 Which my own fair fingers wrought,
Shall unfold its nectared treasures
 To thy lips all smoking hot.

"Ha! I see thy brow is clearing,
 Lustre flashes from thine eyes;
To thy lips I see the moisture
 Of anticipation rise.
Hark! the dinner bell is sounding!"
 "Only wait one moment, Jane:
I'll be dressed, and down, before you
 Can get up the, iced champagne!"

The Husband's Petition.

COME hither, my heart's darling,
    Come, sit upon my knee,
And listen, while I whisper
    A boon I ask of thee.
You need not pull my whiskers
    So amorously, my dove;
'T is something quite apart from
    The gentle cares of love.

I feel a bitter craving—
    A dark and deep desire,
That glows beneath my bosom
    Like coals of kindled fire.
The passion of the nightingale,
    When singing to the rose,
Is feebler than the agony
    That murders my repose!

Nay, dearest! do not doubt me,
    Though madly thus I speak—
I feel thy arms about me,
    Thy tresses on my cheek :

I know the sweet devotion
   That links thy heart with mine,—
I know my soul's emotion
   Is doubly felt by thine:

And deem not that a shadow
   Hath fallen across my love:
No, sweet, my love is shadowless,
   As yonder heaven above.
These little taper fingers—
   Ah, Jane! how white they be!—
Can well supply the cruel want
   That almost maddens me.

Thou wilt not sure deny me
   My first and fond request;
I pray thee, by the memory
   Of all we cherish best—
By all the dear remembrance
   Of those delicious days,
When, hand in hand, we wandered
   Along the summer braes:

By all we felt, unspoken,
   When 'neath the early moon,
We sat beside the rivulet,
   In the leafy month of June;
And by the broken whisper
   That fell upon my ear,
More sweet than angel-music,
   When first I woo'd thee, dear!